MOUNTAIN
PEOPLE, PLACES AND WAYS
A SOUTHERN APPALACHIAN SAMPLER

Michael Joslin
Ruth Joslin

The Overmountain Press

JOHNSON CITY, TENNESSEE

INTRODUCTION

These stories were written and the photographs taken between the summer of 1985 and the fall of 1991 for the **Johnson City Press**, a daily newspaper in Johnson City, Tennessee. We present them as a record of what has been and what is now. The people we met, the places we visited, and the ways we learned have shown us the hardiness and integrity of the folks who have settled these mountains, the richness and sustaining power of their environment, and the special culture that has evolved over the years as the people have adapted to their place.

Just as the mountain folk arrange their lives by the progress of the seasons, we have organized the articles by their falling into spring, summer, fall, or winter. One of the special glories of these Southern Appalachians is their seasonal progression, their experiencing a true fall, winter, and spring in a region of the country that has only faint imitations of those seasons. While many tourists seek only the cool mountain summers as a respite from the lowlands' heat and humidity, the year-round resident knows the trials but also the beauties of the other seasons. In part the deep faith of most mountain folks comes from their recognition of God's hand in the wheel of the year and their relative weakness in the face of such power.

We publish this collection in hope that the people and their ways will continue to flourish in their land. Against development and exploitation, we know that the billion-year-old mountains will in the end prevail.

Michael E. Joslin

CONTENTS

SPRING

FALL

WORKING HORSES

BULADEAN, N.C.—When the snow and ice have disappeared from even the most deeply shaded coves, daffodils nod their yellow heads beside today's homes and around long-vanished ones. The singing of birds softens the rooster's early morning crowing.

The land awaits the plow. To most farmers that means cranking up the tractor. To a few hardy mountain farmers it means harnessing their horses, as their fathers did, and their fathers' fathers did.

"Nothing tickles me better than to get a couple of horses and go to plowing," says Howard Burleson, lifelong resident of Buladean. "But it is hard work."

Over a hundred horses have worked with Howard during his better than 60 years of farming the steep fields above Greasy Creek. He knows horses, he loves horses, and he respects their ability to maintain the land.

He admits readily that a tractor can get things done much faster, that a man can plow with a tractor in one hour what a horse does in one day. But he also stresses that speed to a farmer is not the most important factor.

"You can keep your land up with a horse. You can use their manure back on the ground to build the land," he says. "The tractor kills it, ruins the ground. The wheels, then especially the disc, packs it to death.

"And there's no manure from a tractor."

Early each morning this past week Howard has been out with Betty, his Belgian mare, and Bonnie, owned by Ralph Hill, one of the next generation with plans to keep the tradition alive along with his land.

"You don't learn it overnight," Howard says with a laugh. "It takes a right smart bit of time to learn to work horses."

He and Ralph have worked many times together in the steep fields and on the rich bottomland under the Roan. For at least another generation, the horse and plow will be a familiar part of the landscape along with the tobacco patches on the tilted mountainsides.

"Most people have let all their land grow up that they can't tractor. They're not tending it anymore," says Howard with a disapproving shake of his head. "People have gotten lazy, won't work what they can't tractor."

A reassuring link with a simpler time is the sight of Howard and Ralph stepping along behind two powerful horses on a cool spring morning. As the sun rises and the chill turns to sweat, the steady plodding establishes a timeless rhythm.

It is good that some farms continue to operate organically, the pulse of the earth throbbing with that of man and beast across the generations.

Ralph Hill (left) and Howard Burleson plow a field.

WILDFLOWERS

As winter fights the last skirmishes of its inevitably losing battle with spring, mountain forests and meadows reawaken with an explosion of wildflowers.

From late March until the bitter days of late autumn, a continuous succession of blossoms adds a gentle beauty to the rugged slopes and crests of the Southern Appalachians. When high mountains still look forbidding, with the stern grays and browns of winter dominating the scattered white puffs of the serviceberry trees with their blossoms, vivid colors of spring already dot the forest floor.

This mountain community supports over 1,400 flowering plants and trees, many of which are rare and endangered. From early in the 18th century, botanists from around the world have journeyed to the Black Mountains, the Roan, the Great Smoky Mountains, and other area ranges to study, collect, and catalog this remarkable profusion of plant life.

Roan Mountain alone has been visited by Andre Michaux, Nuttall, François Michaux, Fraser, Gray, and Curtis, all renowned botanists and scientists.

One of the most intriguing aspects of studying and enjoying the mountain wildflowers is the opportunity to see the seasonal succession unfold in less than a day by walking from a valley floor to a mountain peak. In making such a climb, one moves through vegetation zones ranging from that of North Carolina's Piedmont to that of central Canada.

While valley floors show the luxuriant foliage and abundant blossoms of late May or June, the highest peaks may still hold bare-branched trees and only the earliest spring flowers.

Some of these early flowers appear in mid-March on the lower slopes. Bloodroot with its snowy-white petals, spring beauty with its red-striped petals, larkspur with its bright purple flowers, violets of a wide variety of hues, tiny bluets, simple toothwort, and the demurely white hepatica are a few of these early bloomers hidden on the mountain forest floors.

As the season advances, the wildflowers continue to burgeon in ever-increasing numbers. Joining the flowers on the ground are those of a variety of trees. Dogwood, redbud, serviceberry, silverbell, tulip poplar, crab apple, and other escaped and native fruit trees enliven with their blossoms the still-winter-stripped woods.

On the forest floor, the Trillium family—wake robin, Catesby's trillium, nodding trillium, painted trillium, and large-flowered trillium—bring color and delicate beauty to April.

They are joined by widespread wild strawberry, fancifully shaped

Dutchman's breeches and squirrel corn, red bleeding heart, yellow trout lily, Mayapple, and chickweed, among others.

May and June bring with them the rich, profuse colors of the blooming rhododendron, flame azalea, and mountain laurel.

Early explorer-botanist William Bartram's famous description of the flame azalea captures well its effect:

"The epithet fiery, I annex to this most celebrated species of azalea as being expressive of the appearance of its flowers, which are in general the colour of the finest red lead, orange and bright gold, as well as yellow and cream colour; . . . the clusters of the blossoms cover the shrubs in such incredible profusion on the hill sides, that suddenly opening to view from dark shades, we are alarmed with the apprehension of the hill being set on fire."

Throughout the summer and well into the autumn the procession of blossoms continues, ending with the ubiquitous aster as the blazing fall foliage presages the return of winter.

While many mountain sites such as Roan Mountain and the Great Smoky Mountains National Park preserve the wealth of flowering plants, many other areas have lost or are in danger of losing these treasures.

"Because of the delicately balanced adaptation to very specific natural environments, many wildflowers cannot grow in habitats that have been altered or disturbed, nor can they compete with the plants of the more weedy and introduced species that rapidly invade the vast areas of land opened or altered by the machines of man," writes C. Ritchie Bell in **Wild Flowers of North Carolina**.

Development destroys many acres of wildflower habitats each year. Even our national forests' many wildflower areas are threatened. The replanting of clearcut hardwood forests with white pines dooms many hundreds of acres in the Cherokee National Forest alone, where one-third of the harvested hardwood forest is replanted in pine.

For many thousands of years, perhaps millions, the gray and white bleakness of the winter forest has given way to the rich profusion of color that the wildflowers bring with spring. While enjoying this natural bounty of beauty, remember how delicately nature's scale is balanced.

Take from the forest only pictures, memories, and the resolve to maintain our natural treasures for the generations to come.

Lady's Slipper

Painted Trillium

Large Flowered Trillium

BRUCE GREENE: MOUNTAIN MUSICIAN

CELO, N.C.—Few sounds are sweeter than mountain music floating on a warm spring breeze. The clear vibrations of a fiddle's strings, the mellow tones of a much-used voice rendering an old tune, and the hum of sun-warmed bees compose the living breath of Appalachia.

Working to preserve that vital essence is Bruce Greene, who lives on the eastern side of the Black Mountains, under towering Cattail Peak. Greene has spent twenty years or more learning, playing, and recording the musical heritage of these southern mountains.

Starting in the early 1970s, Greene sought out old-time musicians in Kentucky. He would learn their songs and techniques, the stories behind the songs, and then record these old fiddlers and singers.

Recently he has begun his research and learning in the western counties of North Carolina, primarily in Mitchell and Yancey Counties.

"There's not too many old-time musicians around anymore. They're mostly dead. When I find one, I like to talk to him and learn about his life and how the music was handed down. Then I record him," Greene said.

"I always was doing it first to learn the music myself. I don't like the idea of being a 'collector'—it changes the relationship. I want to learn the music and learn about it and then try to preserve it," he said.

Preservation of this part of the mountain heritage is important to Greene, who has seen most of the last generation of traditional musicians die as this century has moved to its end.

"Sooner or later people are going to realize that they had ways which gave them a cultural identity. But if those ways are lost, there will be no way to recover that identity.

"Something like the music is especially threatened. You can't look in an old barn and find it, the way you can find an old plow or piece of harness. The music must be passed down from generation to generation," he said.

He cites as an example of the fragility of this part of the culture an old lady he visited this past November. He talked with her and recorded her songs. A week later she had a stroke and died.

"If I hadn't been there, her music and the tradition it held would have been lost forever," Greene said, mingling relief and sadness.

From his research and conversations with the old timers, Greene has found that in the 1920s and '30s the opening of the mountains to the mass culture of the United States made many of the young people turn away from their traditions.

Bruce Greene

"They looked at the old-timers, the ones depicted as hillbillies, and said, 'We don't want to be like them. We want to be modern.' In one generation the tradition of the old music largely died out. It wasn't handed down," he said.

Also, when the graphophone first appeared in the mountains the neighbors that had formerly gathered to play and sing together began to gather to listen to the wax recordings.

"It was much easier to flick a switch than to learn to play the fiddle, and they would feel 'modern,' " he said with a sad shake of his head.

When the telephone appeared, the gatherings often became party line listening over the wires, so that even the communal spirit suffered. The graphophone would be placed near the mouthpiece, so neighbors would have piped-in music.

Today the attitudes towards the traditional mountain culture have changed in many ways. Many of the descendants of the early settlers and many of the newcomers see the value in the mountain culture and romanticize it.

"That's part of the problem," said Greene. "Most don't know what the true culture was. Part of what I'm trying to do is document that culture and put it in the local libraries where people can listen to the old musicians."

One of Greene's favorite stories concerns a contest between two fiddlers in Eastern Kentucky in the early 1800s. Each tried to prove that he knew more tunes than the other.

"Jim Flannery was one, and the other was a Day, I believe. They played all day and into the night. Both ran out at the same time. They decided to sleep on it and take up again in the morning.

"Jim Flannery dreamed he was being chased by a bear who played a fiddle. He woke up and remembered the tune. He won the contest playing it. The fiddlers called it **Flannery's Dream**," said Greene, taking up his fiddle and bringing **Flannery's Dream** alive once again.

Another favorite story is about the fiddler who got religion and gave up the fiddle.

"Any music that isn't religious they call 'love songs,' and a lot won't play the 'love songs.' They also call it 'devil's music.'

"After about a year the fiddler got the itch to play so bad he couldn't stand it. He decided it would be okay if he just played religious music, so he reached under the bed and dragged out his fiddle. He tuned it up," said Greene with a smile.

"When he took it up to play, the first tune that came out was **Betty Baker**, definitely not a religious song. So he broke the fiddle over the

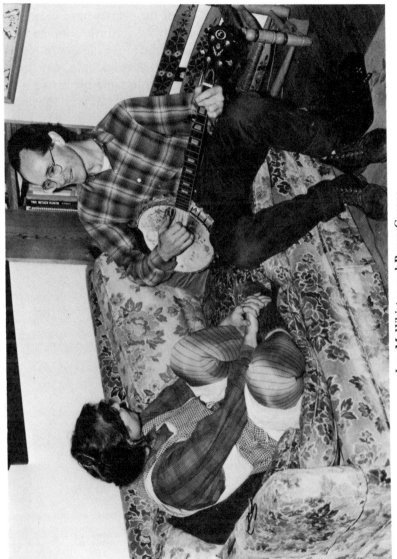

Loy McWhirter and Bruce Greene

head of the bed so he'd never be tempted again,'' said Greene, who then took up his fiddle and played the lively **Betty Baker**.

Aiding Greene in his project is his partner Loy McWhirter. When she joins her voice to his in sweet harmony, the loss to the culture when radio and mechanical reproduction replaced the living music becomes clear. The song haunts the ear long after the sounds have faded.

Although he has applied for a grant from the North Carolina Arts Council to help with the recording, so far the project has been totally Greene's own. He works as a carpenter and does odd jobs, as well as performing whenever he can, to finance his life and his work.

There is no doubt that he knows the worth of his endeavor. The peace that settles on him as he picks up a fiddle or banjo to play, or sings an heirloom song, passes understanding. And that peace spreads from his sunny porch to the looming Black Mountains on the widening ripples of the sound.

NATURE CENTER

ASHEVILLE, N.C.—"An educational experience"—it's a cliche that immediately turns off most of us, especially school children.

Yet at the Western North Carolina Nature Center, that kind of experience is so rewarding and downright enjoyable that the hours spent in education pass rapidly and pleasurably, leaving the learner hungry for more.

Who doesn't enjoy watching playful otters frolic exuberantly in a splashful game of tag?

Or who wouldn't laugh when a pair of miniature goats hop, skip, and jump over to nibble his fingers?

Who objects to playing simple, yet challenging games that entertained Indian children or those pastimes the offspring of pioneers enjoyed?

These kind of smile-inducers are the essence of the center, and such activities abound on the banks of the Swannanoa River where Buncombe County maintains this center of environmental education.

"We're a regional center, here to interpret the natural environment. We show how the environment affects people, and how people affect the environment," says Dan Lazar, naturalist for the center.

"Our mission is man's interaction with his environment, past and present," echoes Zack Allen, director of the center. "Our exhibits interweave all phases of this interaction so that through knowledge will come understanding."

Many come to sample that knowledge and gain the understanding.

In the past year nearly 60,000 visitors have come to the center, 20,000 of whom were school children. While most of these were from Western North Carolina and East Tennessee, people from 34 states and nine foreign countries—from Europe, South America, and Asia—visited the center.

In addition there are visits to area schools.

"We have an outreach program that goes to each of the schools throughout the year. Each child sees programs six times before he leaves the sixth grade," Lazar says.

An abundance of exhibits and displays fills the four acres of land. The map and guide distributed by the center lists 26 different things to see and do, from the cougar cage to a passive solar composting toilet.

Exhibits of Indian culture and pioneer living are in the entrance building. Actual artifacts of the time are displayed beside hands-on demonstrations of such activities as Indian corn grinding and pioneer shingle making.

In the main exhibit building are archeological exhibits, aquatic reptiles and fish, a section lit by red lights for observing nocturnal animals, and an area for the care and rehabilitation of injured animals and birds.

Leaving the buildings, you are greeted by a unique medley of sounds. The cougar's harsh growl, the timber wolf's deep, haunting howl, the chattering of guinea fowl, the raucous honks of pilgrim geese, the baaing of goats and sheep, and an occasional screech from the strutting peacocks remind you that your environment is more that what you see or touch.

Predators such as cougars, foxes, raccoons, and wildcats show visitors a part of their environment seldom glimpsed. The roles of these animals are explained, as is their fate at the hands of man. And questions are raised, such as "How will our forests change now that the cougar is gone?"

Next is the Wildlife Habitat Demonstration Trail that shows how each of us can help provide homes for the animals that are dispossessed by the ever-increasing shopping malls and housing developments.

The Treetop Nature Trail travels by boardwalk through the upper reaches of trees to expose everyone to a part of the environment that is always there but seldom experienced by such earth-dwelling creatures as ourselves.

Underneath the boardwalk a herd of white-tailed deer roams with wild turkeys, and next door a black bear plays.

At the end of the boardwalk are the farm grounds with enough animals and demonstrations to fill a day.

The children's barnyard displays a sign, "Please feel free to pet the animals." And the animals reinforce the sign by seeking attention.

There's Christopher, a 21-year-old Sicilian donkey. "He's so old he don't know nothing but being friendly," says Frank Teague, who oversees the farm exhibits.

Teague himself should be considered part of the exhibit, a major part. His 87 years sit lightly on him, and he is as representative of life on the farm as are the goats, pigs, and composting bins. His homely wisdom uttered in laconic comments identify him as a mountain farmer from way back.

The most unique exhibit of the center is the World Underground, a recently opened look at the fascinating life that populates the ground under our feet.

A series of dioramas takes the visitor into the earth, showing life does not end at ground level. A cutaway view reveals earthworms, mice, groundhogs, and other denizens of the subsurface.

Mountain Lion

One pair of dioramas in the World Underground contrasts the life of the forest with that of the tobacco field. The abundance of the former next to the sterility of the latter provides a lesson a million words couldn't.

Education happens imperceptibly here.

"We try not to preach at all here," Lazar says. "We present the information as clearly as we can through natural artifacts and exhibits. They tell the story."

And there are many versions of the story—too many to introduce here. The aviary with red-tailed hawks, owls, a golden eagle; the turtle pond with ducks and frogs; the wet meadow; the demonstration gardens; the Mount Mitchell scene; and many more make a one-day visit a full experience and call you back for a better look another time.

The Western North Carolina Nature Center is open from 10 a.m. to 5 p.m. Tuesday through Saturday and 1-5 p.m. Sunday. Admission is $1.50 for adults and $1 for children and senior citizens. There are also group rates available.

For information call (704) 298-5600.

The center can be reached from the Blue Ridge Parkway and Interstate 240 by following the signs to its location on N.C. highway 81.

But don't tell the kids it's an educational experience.

Otter

ALPINE INN

LITTLE SWITZERLAND, N.C.—When you first see the Alpine Inn, it appears that only magic keeps the hotel perched on the eastern edge of the Blue Ridge. It juts dramatically off the precipitous side of Grassy Mountain a short distance from the Blue Ridge Parkway to overlook the mountains and valleys that diminish down to the piedmont many miles away.

"A lot of people are afraid to stay here. While someone in the carload will like our looks, another person might be too afraid to even step out on our balconies," says Bill Cox, who with his wife Sharon Smith owns and runs the 58-year-old inn.

"But we are really quite secure. The building is supported by steel I-beams that run through the mountain and under the road. Plus we have 25 locust trunks for added support," he says.

Because of its unique situation, the Alpine Inn provides an unusual environment for visitors.

The main lodge wraps around a large poplar, which seems to spring up through the middle of the building. The balconies hang over the treetops so that instead of looking up to see the birds and blossoms, guests look out or down.

While Bill and Sharon are busy getting their inn prepared for the summer rush, catbirds, cardinals, scarlet tanagers and other birds sing, call, and claim territory all around to establish nesting rights for their summer home.

One cardinal is back for a repeat stay.

"Every morning a cardinal comes to my car and pecks at the rear-view mirror. He was here last year, and he's back this year," says Bill.

This is only the second year for Sharon and Bill, too. They were school teachers in Columbia, South Carolina. Last year they decided to try something new.

"It was the middle of September, 1985. We both had just begun another semester and were worn out with struggles with students and administrations at our schools. One night we said, 'Let's see if we can find a small motel in the mountains to buy,'" says Sharon.

"The next morning I walked to the newsstand and bought an Asheville newspaper, and there was the ad," says Bill. "It did seem like one of those things there just for us."

"It said, 'small mountain motel for sale,' and the price was just a little more than we could scrape up, so we looked into it," adds Sharon.

"We sold everything, our house and stuff, quit our jobs in the middle of the school year, and became innkeepers. I wrote my letter of resignation to the principal on Alpine Inn stationery," finishes Bill with a laugh.

After a winter of repairs, refurbishing, and refurnishing, Bill and Sharon opened for business in April, 1986. They've maintained a unique style to fit the unusual qualities of their establishment.

"We don't have TVs in the rooms. We have a couple we'll let someone use if they want, but most people don't want one. They come here to enjoy the mountains, to sit on the balconies, relaxing and soaking in the sights and sounds of nature." says Bill.

"People comment that all the rooms are unique. Accessories and decorations are left free, not bolted or chained in place. We give our clientele the benefit of the doubt," he adds. "You don't have a bunch of thugs dropping in off the Parkway to enjoy the view."

Like the cardinal back for the spring, many of the guests are repeat customers. The Alpine Inn's offerings are not commonly found, and visitors who like its style tend to return.

"One man came three times last summer with his family. He always stayed in room #9. Once he came and that room was unavailable. He was most upset, but we talked him into taking a chance on the room underneath. He grumbled but accepted. Now he insists on that room. He likes the shower nozzle better," says Bill.

Word of mouth is their prinicipal form of advertising.

"You can't sum up our attractions in an ad. The view and atmosphere defy description. So, we let our visitors talk their friends into trying us on trust. The right person will love us and what we have to offer, and people don't send friends who would rather be entertained by night club acts and wide-screen televisions," says Bill.

Simple mountain pleasures are what the Inn offers. The sunrise attracts a lot of attention.

"A pretty good percentage of the guests get up for it. It's hard to ignore when that morning sun climbs over the mountains and shines in your window," he says.

Open the year-round, most of the Alpine Inn's business comes in the summer through the fall. August with its cool mountain nights and October with its brilliant foliage attract the most visitors from the lowlands; but a steady flow of guests comes through as long as the Blue Ridge Parkway is open. When the winter snows shut down the Parkway, only an occasional tourist comes by.

Daily lodging rates begin at $28, and for $3 guests can enjoy the Balcony Breakfast. A typical menu includes home-baked breads, fruit, jam and jellies, boiled eggs, fruit juice and coffee served on the sunrise-lit balcony.

The Alpine Inn is located one mile off the Blue Ridge Parkway. Exit milepost 334 and proceed west on Highway 226A. Reservations can be made by calling (704) 765-5380.

Bring a book, camera and binoculars, but leave the dancing shoes home.

MOUNTAIN COOKING

BULADEAN, N.C.—On **Hee Haw,** it was always "What's for supper, Grandpa?" I used to wonder why Grandpa Jones would get such a big response when he'd run down his rhymed list of food.

After sitting down to dinner with Verndeannia Hughes I realize that Grandpa Jones' menu is funny because it is so true to life—it simply calls to mind pure mountain eating.

Born and raised in the Western North Carolina Mountains, Verndeannia carries on a cooking tradition which has been passed from generation to generation.

"I never thought of it as mountain cooking. I just thought of it as what we could cook with what we had put up. We've always been able to put up most of what we needed. It's the whole way of life up here," said Verndeannia as she stirred the shuck beans, or leather britches as some people call them.

Last summer Verndeannia dried the shuck beans from her garden on a screen in the sun, the way her mother used to do. She still prepares and stores the same foods her mother and grandmother did, though she sometimes "puts it up" differently.

Verndeannia, like most women in the mountains these days, mixes modern know-how with handed down knowledge to do much of what her foremothers did. Freezers, pressure cookers, electric stoves and microwave ovens have replaced the more tedious drying, all-day cooking and woodstove loading.

"Momma would store her beans in a sack in a dry place. I bag mine up and put them in the freezer," she said.

So, what **was** for dinner last Saturday?

Well...ham hocks and shuck beans, boiled cabbage and corn bread, ham-seasoned potatoes and buttermilk biscuits, creamed corn and skillet-fried country ham, sauerkraut, coleslaw, apple butter, homemade raspberry jelly and blackberry cobbler.

Yum, yum!

Most of what was on the table was raised in the Hughes' own garden. Last year the family didn't keep any hogs, so the ham was from the store and from "Pete"—Rosalea Hughes, a sister-in-law to Verndeannia.

They don't have cows right now, either, so the buttermilk was store-bought, too.

"I was laughing with my sister the other day. When Momma would send us to the store, she'd say, 'Buy me some sugar, meal, flour, coffee and snuff.' That was all we'd have to buy. The rest we'd raised on our own," Verndeannia said, laughing.

Besides shopping differently nowadays, Verndeannia also cooks differently. She heated the corn, which she had scraped from the cob and frozen last fall, in her microwave oven. The compact modern appliance now sits in the same corner where a wood cook stove once stood.

"Twenty years ago I got rid of my wood stove, but I used it right on 'til then. Wood stove's better cookin'. With electricity you cook faster, you tend to hurry it up," she explained.

Standing in her large, modern kitchen you immediately realize that Verndeannia doesn't have to put up food for the winter or continue to cook traditional meals anymore. She has plenty of money to buy prepared, frozen meals at the grocery store which would take less effort.

"I keep on cooking this way because it is the food my family grew up with. It became their favorite food," she said.

Some of the changes in the way Verndeannia keeps and prepares traditional foods come from necessity and some from convenience. Heating the corn took only a minute or two.

She also uses self-rising flour for convenience, but no one would ever complain about it because her biscuits are light and fluffy.

Convenience has nothing to do with Verndeannia's use of the pressure cooker, however. She cooks down her beans and then her ham hock broth in the pressure cooker out of necessity. Her modern electric stove would simply use too much electricity to leave a pot of ham on (without pressure) long enough to make a good broth.

All the same, some of the things on the table were prepared just as her mother did it. The apple butter was cooked up in an iron cauldron over an open fire one cool October day. It was made from apples picked off the trees on the Hughes' Buladean farm.

Although I stood and watched Verndeannia make the entire meal, giving recipes for what she prepared is difficult. She is perfectly at ease in her kitchen, using no measuring cups and no recipe books.

"Before I went to bed last night I put my shuck beans in to soak. This morning I rinsed them off and put water over to cover and added the pork bone," she began.

The shuck beans measured out at about 2½ to 3 quarts.

After the beans had cooked for an hour in the pressure cooker, Verndeannia removed them from the heat and poured them into another pot which was then put over a medium heat. She then started her pork broth by putting two pieces of ham hock and three or four cups of water into the pressure cooker for one half an hour.

While the broth cooked she quartered a large potful of potatoes and put them on to boil. At this point she turned on the already prepared cabbage so that it could begin to boil.

Next Verndeannia prepared corn bread and biscuits by recipes that seemed to be part of an Appalachian consciousness, rather than from some personal memory. If you aren't tapped into that consciousness, she said the recipes on the bag would do. She used store-bought butter-milk in both breads.

The corn bread went into the oven just as the ham broth finished, so she quickly added a cup of broth to her beans, one to the cabbage, and one to the potatoes. She also pulled the meat from the ham bones and added it to the potatoes, then returned the vegetables to the heat to simmer.

Next she opened a home-can of already sweetened blackberries, poured them into a baking pan, and covered them with half of the biscuit dough. To cover the berries she shaped the dough into three-inch, flat rounds, each with a small hole in the middle. She also delicately formed biscuits with her hands, and put them into another pan.

After the cobbler and the biscuits joined the corn bread in the oven, Verndeannia skillet-fried three large slabs of ham. As the ham was finishing, she popped the homemade cream-style corn in the microwave for less than two minutes. Miraculously, it seemed to me, everything was done at the same time.

Just as what she cooks is a part of her whole way of life, how she prepares it fits smoothly into Verndeannia's way of living. Verndeannia is a wonderful example of an Appalachian woman—everything she does has a harmony and balance.

CHIMNEYS

BULADEAN, N.C.—The landscape of Southern Appalachia has changed greatly in the past 50 years. Thousands of acres of cropland and pasture that once supported hardworking farming families have reverted to the woodlands that covered these mountains before the white man came with his axe and plow.

One of the most enduring signs of the way of life that has passed are the stone chimneys that proclaim, "Here was a house, a home where life and love endured hard work and cold winters."

They often stand alone, sometimes in tall woods that have effaced all other signs of farm and family, sometimes on the edge of old roads that have become paths for deer and other forest creatures.

The more recently abandoned sites retain the shape of house and farmstead, the heavy log walls slowly subsiding to soil, resistant locust fenceposts outlining former animal lots, pastures, and corn fields.

The stone chimney is almost always the last functioning part of a once-vital farmstead.

There is a story about each—and many stories about some—of these clay and stone towers whose existence testifies to the work of the handy mountain man who has returned to dust. Even the crumbled piles of stone have a tale to tell.

One such chimney whose stack had fallen in with the roof that once surrounded it whispers a fortune teller's story. In the ruin you can see the remnants of her taste for a pretty touch—the arch above the firebox is a line of red bricks, bright in the midst of the grey stone.

There are those who still remember.

"That was Miz Slagle's place. She told everybody's fortune," says Pauline Street, who recently celebrated her 80th birthday.

"We would walk from Buladean up to her cove to have our fortune told. She didn't charge nothing, but we'd give her a quarter or fifty cents. About all the money she ever got was from fortune telling. I remember she had these old time chairs with hickory bark bottoms.

"She read coffee grounds for me, best I can recollect. It was a long time ago," says Mrs. Street.

"I seen her back before I went into the army. It must have been in the '30s," says Pauline's husband, Paul Street.

"She came up to the house way back at the head of the creek. She just looked at my hand and told me a few things," he says.

"She told me I'd be sick a lot in my life. I've been sick for the 40 years since the war.

This 1937 chimney still stands at the top of Beans Creek.

"She told me I'd come into some money, and I've got a right smart bit of money," he says.

"She told me a lot about women, but I don't remember what right now," Paul says, sliding a look across the room to his wife.

How many hopes rose before the coffee grounds were dashed into that fireplace? How many old folks still glance at their palms and hear Miz Slagle's voice echoing faintly in their ears? How long before that chimney will be the only memorial of her life?

High upon the Buladean side of Roan Mountain other chimneys tell a tale of a whole community of farmers that has passed into the mists of time which can be as obscuring as the heavy clouds that often shroud the mountain. Fortunately there are those still alive who remember that life.

"I lived up there for more than 20 years," says Taylor Hughes, who now lives down on the valley floor. "It was a good place to live."

A description of one site or another sends him back to times when horses and sledges carried families and goods about the steep roads, when a trip even to Buladean at the bottom of the mountain was an event. Self-sufficiency created a life in which isolation didn't mean deprivation.

"We had a lot of stock up there. And there was a lot of game. I remember walking through some bushes and seeing four or five pheasants just a-sitting there all together," he says.

But things change.

"Folks died off or moved out. It's hard to get up there in a car. I remember having to walk out of there in one snow that was that deep," he says, holding his hand above his knee.

Today the forest gathers back a bit of the farmsteads each year. But the chimneys still stand to tell of a time when all a man needed to heat his home was a strong back, work-hardened hands, rocks which the mountains provided in abundance, and a bank of clay.

Many such memorials dot the mountains and coves of Western North Carolina and East Tennessee. To me they are as evocative as such old world ruins as the Coliseum, and more pleasing, for they tell of simple virtues and homely joys as well as hard struggles. Ozymandias' pride is not here.

Close-up of the chimney box

TWO TREES: INDIAN MEDICINE MAN

OLD FORT, N.C.—At first thought, it seems an unlikely place to seek medical advice—a small wooden pyramid set behind an aging frame house on a rough dirt road at the foot of the Blue Ridge.

And at first glance the practitioner seems an unlikely man for large numbers of sufferers to trust and praise—Chief Two Trees, a Cherokee Indian wearing blue jeans, cowboy boots, and a plaid shirt.

Yet the steady parade of the sore and sick keeps coming to this secluded place near the former frontier town of Old Fort, and patient after patient leaves with a sprightlier step and praise on his lips.

A chiropractor from Florida, a factory worker from Rutherfordton, North Carolina, a wealthy businessman from Knoxville, and a poor laborer from the nearby mountains—each is amazed by the skilful hands and knowledgeable eyes of Two Trees.

"I think he's fantastic," says Dr. Joy Bauman of the Bauman Chiropractic Clinic, Panama City, Florida, on her first visit to Two Trees. "I've read about people like this, but I've never met one."

Dr. Bauman arrived with her two sisters, one of whom, 79-year-old Ruby Lowe, has been passing out lately.

"My worst trouble is this ear. Something's wrong and I just fall on the floor," she says.

Two Trees gets her on his table and works over her spine, her neck, and her head.

"You ain't done nothing like this to me," Mrs. Lowe tells her chiropractor sister, who leans closely to learn from the medicine man.

Before they leave, Dr. Bauman has adopted several of the shaman's techniques of spinal adjustment, and all are giggling like school girls. They clutch the list of herbal medicines they are to purchase at a health food store and their bottles of the chief's special mineral water.

Liz Barnett is a worker at the OMC factory in Rutherfordton. She's been coming to Two Trees for some time now.

"I've seen him do fabulous things, and he's helped me out a lot. I first came after I'd had two ribs cut out and was suffering from pain. If I'd a known about him before, I never would have had surgery.

"He's a good teacher. I come up here a lot of times just to sit in on sessions and learn," she says. "He's good, but he tells you that you've got to want to do it yourself. Most of it is left up to you."

The Knoxville businessman with his wife and daughter is more reticent. The two women are willing to talk, but he doesn't want his name or picture in the paper. The family has come here before, and they trust the advice they receive and obtain relief from the spinal adjustments.

But what would his associates think?

Many of the chief's patients are the anonymous poor seeking relief from real pain that finally gets too much for them. Some arrive twisted and bent from the aches that shoot through them. Bones pop and joints crack under Two Tree's manipulations, then the patient stands and walks to see how successful the treatment has been.

"I wouldn't of thought you could of done something like that," says one old mountain man who has had to be helped into and out of bed for months. He now climbs on and off the table, tentatively at first. But with increasing confidence he pulls on his worn work boots and tromps around.

No receptionist prepares a careful accounting of the bill for each patient. A dusty, gallon mayonnaise jar hides beside Two Tree's chair. "$10 suggested donation" is all it says.

One of his patients, a stooped, middle-aged woman in worn clothes and scuffed shoes is told by the medicine man, "No donations today, darling."

The Knoxville businessman, when he and his family leave loaded with mineral water, herbal remedies, and a special clay mixture, stuffs over $100 into the old jar.

"I'm retired from the Air Force. This here doesn't make a living. By the time a lot of people get here they're broke," says Two Trees.

"I was born into it. My mom, dad, grandparents—all were medicine people, and I just learned as I grew up. Also I have studied at universities around the world."

Two Trees works quickly, using his physical senses to make his diagnosis.

"I look at the eyes, the skin, the way they stand and look," he says.

Then he puts them on his table and feels the spine, the neck, the head, adjusting and manipulating as his hands move along the body.

"The human body has everything to keep us healthy, but we interfere with it. Most of our problems are nutritional ones. Good, wholesome food is just not available to a lot of people today, so they must supplement it with herbs in order to get a balanced diet," he explains.

Two Trees came to the mountains to work on a book and a movie script in what he considered a secluded spot.

"I really came here to write. For five years I traveled all over North and South America visiting with medicine people. I call it a spiritual journey, a journey of confirmation," he says. "One publisher is willing to put up big bucks if I'll start work on the book."

"But here I am, two years and 25,000 visitors [his word for patients] later. Instead of working on the book, I am building a traditional teaching center on some land I acquired up the road.

"As we clear the land we find that it had been used for the same purpose about 400 years ago. Arrowheads, pottery, camp fire remains, medicine pots and pipes are all over the site," Two Trees says with a smile.

The coincidence is no surprise to the shaman who believes that Earth is an organism, as ourselves, and that a harmony must be established between man and his planet.

"What I say to people is not deep, mystical, or secret. Keep your power; grow your garden; be your own spiritual counselor, get help from your minister but stay responsible for yourself; manage your money wisely; refrain from giving the decision-making for every moment of your lives to the government," Two Trees says.

Visitors are welcome on Monday, Tuesday, and Saturday; and if you are traveling from a distance, call ahead to ensure Chief Two Trees will be there. His phone number is 704-668-7368.

"We have a new smoke signal now that I use to keep in touch with other medicine people and my visitors. It's called the telephone," he says with a laugh. "There's nothing new under the sun, just a deeper understanding each time it comes around."

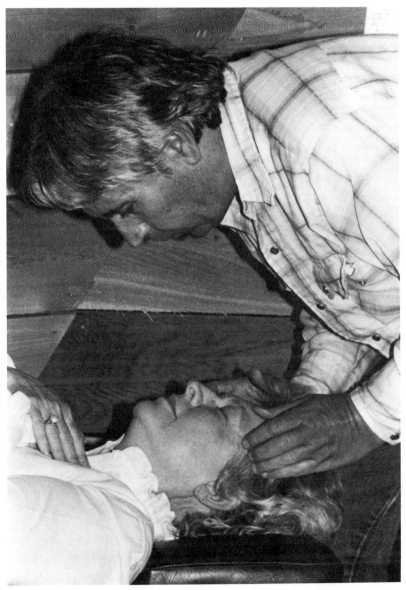

Chief Two Trees uses his healing technique on a visitor.

BULADEAN SOIL

BULADEAN, N.C.—Soil—for most people it's just plain dirt; but for farmers and those they feed, it's as precious as any of our natural resources.

For the past several years, soil scientists have been surveying America's lands to determine what we have of this invaluable resource so that intelligent, knowledgeable decisions can be made about its use.

In Mitchell County, John Allison, team leader of the county soil survey, has "discovered" a new kind of soil, which will be named after the community where it occurs in greatest abundance—the Buladean community under Roan Mountain, snug up against the Tennessee border.

"The tentative name is **Buladean**. The procedure is for the soil scientist that discovers the soil to document it, classify it, then submit it to his superiors with a name. It then works its way up the ladder," says Allison.

"This is the only new soil we've gone ahead with. It's unique because of the combination of the characteristics it possesses. First, it's a colluvial soil, its source material was pulled down by gravity from higher places with water as a lubricant. Here it comes from Roan Mountain.

"While most people think of mountain soil as shallow, this one is particularly deep—10 feet, some places even deeper. It's relatively rock-free with about 50% clay. The surface has a lot of organic matter and is pretty thick," says Allison.

As part of the Mountain Soil Characterization Study, scientists came from Lincoln, Nebraska, to look at three sample pits dug in the Buladean soil and took quantities away with them to study in the laboratory.

One of the pits was dug on Garlan Hughes's farm.

At 71, Hughes has spent his entire life in the shadow of the Roan, farming the soil that has just been "discovered."

"I've plowed just about every foot of this land with a team of horses, so I know what it is," says Hughes, surveying the lush acres around him. "It will grow anything you want in the vegetable line: potatoes, corn, tomatoes, peppers, strawberries, canteloupes. And of course it grows tobacco."

Allison laughs as he hears the old farmer's description.

"I feel like the ornithologist who traveled to a remote place where he discovered a supposedly extinct bird. The natives of the place thought he was crazy to get so excited about a bird that they had known all their lives," says the soil scientist.

"These folks don't call the soils by their proper names, but they do

Garlan Hughes: a Buladean native.

know the differences and have taken care of the various soils.

"People who have lived here for generations know the capabilities better than I do. The evidence of that is the good shape the land is in now after generations and generations of farming," says Allison.

Standing by the escarpment that marks the end of the Buladean colluvium (colluvial soil), Allison and Hughes look up toward massive Roan Mountain which is the source of the soil; then their eyes travel down the valley to stop at an old, red, frame house.

"I was born right there in that house 71 years ago," says the mountain farmer. "It's a long time ago; a short time, too, it seems like. We used to grow things all up the sides of the mountains—used horses and mules, and some used oxen.

"I've kept the ground built up. I keep it clean, put lime on it when it needs, and sow grass as a cover," says Hughes.

"Long before scientists were telling farmers how to care for their land, these folks have been careful of erosion. They've always strip-cropped and sowed a cover crop and put manure on their land," says Allison.

"They're proud of their soil and have tried to keep it the way it started. It's a pleasure for me to walk over well cared for soil rather than the eroded junk I've surveyed before," he adds. "You can see here he's left the steeper land in meadow to prevent erosion."

Mute but powerful evidence of the necessity of the intelligent care of the land by the old Buladean farmers lies on one steep slope coming down from a cove that has recently been cleared by a newcomer to the mountains. Most of the rich soil that once mantled the land there lies at the foot of the slope or is lost silting up Rock Creek that runs at its base.

"I mapped that area as non-soil," says Allison. "After a soil has been disturbed beyond its rooting depth we don't call it soil."

One of the soil scientist's concerns is that, through his identification, the peculiarly fertile and productive soil in Buladean will be kept in farming rather than be developed.

"Buladean is prime farmland, and the soil survey will indicate this. Prime farmland throws up red flags to any developers in government programs," Allison says. "However, right now anyone who can buy the land can bulldoze it. Then we would all lose."

Knowing what resources are available and planning how to use them wisely are important to the future of the farmers of Buladean, as well as to the county, state, nation and world as a whole.

The discoveries of the Soil Survey are vital to this process, and contributing to those discoveries are the shrewd farmers whose knowledge of the land is second to none.

LEES-MCRAE COLLEGE TOWER

BANNER ELK, N.C.—While Notre Dame has its Golden Dome, and ETSU has its Minidome, Lees-McRae College has its Tower to serve as focus and hallmark.

Made from mountain fieldstone and constructed by native mountain workers, the tower has undergone several changes and served a variety of roles since its construction in 1924.

Originally the tower was needed to bring water to the campus and the surrounding community.

"The water supply had been from two springs up on Beech Mountain's slopes above the village. They were not sufficient, so my brother, Edgar Tufts, Jr. who was president, got an engineer to come to see about the water supply," said Margaret Tufts Neal, daughter of college founder Edgar Tufts, recently.

The engineer decided to have water piped to a reservoir on Hemlock Hill, and from there to a metal tower on the ridge.

"Well, you know what a big metal tower looks like, so my brother asked if they could cover it with stone," said Mrs. Neal.

Sending out brochures entitled, "Rocks by the Ton," the elder Edgar Tufts had in 1917 solicited contributions to supply the material for new buildings on campus.

"There are tons and tons of stone lying on the slopes of the mountainsides that surround Banner Elk. They have every shape and size imaginable. They were put there ages ago by the hand of the creator for some good purpose," he wrote.

He added that for $4.00, one ton of native stone with cement and labor could be turned into walls. He hoped to appeal to everyone's eye for an extraordinary bargain.

Finley Townsend, a local man whose enthusiasm matched his giant frame, was appointed foreman and chief rock mason. Working with the rocks deposited over the millenia from the surrounding mountains, he directed the construction.

"Mr. Townsend was very creative, a complete mountain man. He had very little education, but he was creative with rock work.

"He said to my brother, 'Mr. Tufts, I want to make this as beautiful as Solomon's Temple.' Of course, I'm sure that he never knew what Solomon's Temple looked like, but that was his idea of beauty," said Mrs. Neal.

Signs of Townsend's eye for beauty are a stone star above the door of the building and decorative rock-and-brick-filled windows high on the Tower. Also, the ground floor glass windows are tastefully framed by stonework arches.

"He put red brick in a primitive design because mountain people greatly admired red brick because it was so unusual in the area then," said Mrs. Neal.

The Tower held 25,000 gallons of water when completed, and became the hallmark for the campus.

While it has remained a distinguishing feature of the Lees-McRae College campus, the water tower has passed through several incarnations to become today the Bell Tower.

Graduating senior Geoff Hurdle has heard the chimes of the Tower over his years at Lees-McRae, and as his senior project has undertaken to research the history of the building and to have it placed on the state study list for eligibility to become part of the National Register of Historic Places.

"On my arrival in 1987 the Tower was just that, a tower. Soon into my sophomore year, I was inducted into an organization known as The Order of the Tower," Hurdle said.

"I started associating myself with the Tower. If I was going to meet someone, I usually would have them meet me at the Tower. I asked questions about the purpose and history of the Tower. I became, for some reason, enthralled with the Tower," he said.

In his research, Hurdle has traced the history of the tower, and from this information has started the application process for placing the building on the National Register of Historic Places.

After "its retirement as a water storage shed," the Tower served as a lookout tower during World War II, a radio station, a meeting place, and perhaps as a beauty parlor and an ice storage shed, according to Hurdle.

Signs of its use as a lookout tower are several iron poles sticking above the roof. These poles once supported a cover under which the Civil Defense watchers took shelter as they scanned the skies for German bombers that might be on their way to the Oak Ridge Atomic site.

Mrs. Neal has a vague recollection of its beauty parlor days.

"Once a girl wanted to run a beauty parlor there, but it didn't last. It was just a temporary attempt," she said.

The radio station WLMC broadcast from the second floor during the late 1950s and possibly the early '60s, and the Order of the Tower met there for several years.

The "chimes," which are really loudspeakers broadcasting a tape, were donated by Mrs. Sadie Faw in the 1950s. Their soothing tones

Watertower

remind everyone on campus of the Tower's presence every day.

Hearing them brings a smile to Geoff Hurdle's face. He has completed his project and sent the application off to be reviewed. His work is done. The Tower's role at Lees-McRae will continue.

Geoff Hurdle gives his report about the tower.

Stone star above door

Lower window with stone arch

INDIAN EXCAVATION

BURNSVILLE, N.C.—The children at the Cane River Middle School have watched a drama played out behind their school this year. An archaeological dig and a ceremonial Indian encampment, with the resulting cultural clash, have brought history and abstract ideas into vivid reality.

Appropriately, the conflict has centered on the football field. It has been played out in a civilized fashion and resolved with fair play.

"Almost a year ago, last summer, we were putting in a new septic system. The leach field was to be under the football field. When they bulldozed the field, the people found a skeleton," said Phillip Ray, assistant principal of the school.

"We were called and told that an Indian burial had been disturbed in the construction," said David Moore, staff archaeologist for the North Carolina Department of Cultural Resources.

Upon investigating, Moore discovered that an entire Indian village lay buried behind the school and was partially covered by the football field. He dates occupation sometime between 1300 to 1500 A.D., probably for not more than a generation.

"We are conducting the excavation to try to study the way that Indians lived here 500 years ago," said Moore.

"It's a wonderful opportunity for the students to see the archaeological dig," said Ray.

They have also learned something about the native Americans and their values. On April 23, a ceremonial campsite beside the field was established by Indians.

"We aren't here to protest; we came here to pray and participate in ceremonies. We will always honor our ancestors," said Bill Thomas, a Shawnee-Delaware, Creek, Cherokee, "and a little white, too."

"Most of all I'm just a human being," he said.

Rogers Clinch, an Oklahoma Cherokee who lives in the nearby Beelog Community of Yancey County, called attention to the dig and rounded up support from all over for the native rights concerning ancestral bones.

"This is the first time the issue has come up in Yancey County. The local people have not really expressed themselves officially on the issue, but countless people have come up to me to say they're glad we won, although there has been no winning or losing" said Clinch.

The problem is fundamental—how to reconcile one culture's emphasis on rationality and factual information with the other's reliance on intuition and spiritual tradition.

What has been resolved favorably for the local Indians concerns the removal of bones from the site last year.

"The body found last summer was taken to Wake Forest University, but will be reinterred here eventually," said Ray.

"The plan from nine months ago was to wait to hear from the Eastern Cherokees, and that's appropriate both legally and morally. The protest we acknowledge, but they can't speak legally for the remains. That is the right of the Eastern Band," said Moore.

"Legally we could have removed them [the bones], but at this point we are planning to leave them in their present position. We are not even going to excavate them," he said.

Using mainly volunteers, Moore directs the slow work of discovery at the site.

"This was a whole village with a stockade around it. Inside, the houses were 20 feet in diameter, made of posts set in the ground, then branches were wrapped between them, then they were packed with mud to form the walls. They didn't have cupboards but dug pits or holes to store food and cooking vessels," said Moore.

"The small dark circles are each a post, so you can see where the houses were and where the stockade was. One of the palisades ran right through the middle of our pit. The large dark circles are the fire pits," he said, pointing into the site.

"The houses were 20 feet in diameter and made of posts with branches wrapped between them and packed with mud. The dead were buried within the village. The Cherokee ancestors of this time period buried people inside or just outside their houses, so there are no specific 'burial sites.'" added the archaeologist.

Digging in the fire pits, volunteers have found bones, pottery fragments, and other signs of Indian life. A series of screens has been set up to wash the excavated dirt through to save anything that remains on the screen.

While the dig proceeds to investigate the dwelling sites and the fire pits of the former village, the modern Indians will continue their ceremonial presence.

"Raising the consciousness of the school children and the local community is part of our goal," said Clinch.

"This is part of our teachings—to honor our ancestors, as well as our children and grandchildren and children unborn who will be inheriting this world," said Thomas.

Part of their encampment is a ceremonial sweat lodge where the Indians show their reverence for the earth, "our Mother," Thomas said. They

Bill Thomas shows a sweat lodge built for rituals near the dig site.

also fly their colors and offer tobacco tithes to the four directions.

Drumbeats, "the heartbeats of the Mother," echo across the fields between the woods and the school, while a sacred fire burns steadily in the camp.

"We will stay as long as the dig goes on. We are here to demonstrate against the desecration of the Indians, the civil war dead, the blacks buried in unmarked graves—all the dead, and the desecration of the planet. Everyday is Earth Day for us," said Thomas.

"I've approached the mayor and the county commissioners to endorse a plan to hold an annual event to commemorate this site, to bring unity and respect. What better place could there be than here on a school site to make students aware of the different cultures and our beliefs," he said.

Not the least important lesson the children are learning is that disputes can be settled peacefully. No scalps have been taken and no tepees burned. And the bones will rest in peace.

Archeologist David Moore speaks to elementary students beside the dig site.

RAISING WOLVES

LINVILLE, N.C.—"O-oooh!" The eerie howl of the wolf sent shivers down the backs of pioneers isolated among the mountains of East Tennessee and Western North Carolina. For years these settlers hunted the eastern timber wolf and finally succeeded in wiping them out.

Ironically, now that these native wolves are gone forever from their former home, many people want them back to keep as pets. The animals that spread terror are now sought as unusual additions to the domestic setting.

Who wants them?

"You'd be surprised," says Dr. Barbara Coggin, a Linville veterinarian who raises wolf hybrids for sale. "A lot are executive types from large cities; a lot are yuppies; some are people who live on farms. One lady works with the humane society, and I had a 65-year-old woman from Long Island buy a female.

"I mainly sell away from here. I have to fly them out," she says. "I advertise in the *Washington Post, New York Daily News, Miami Herald*, and *Atlanta Constitution*. I describe them as wolf/malamute hybrids with a pure wolf father.

"That's all you have to say, and boy, they'll call," she said.

The selling price is not cheap. The hybrid cubs go for $900 each.

"I hope the price makes people realize what they are buying. Getting a wolf hybrid is a 14-year commitment, and I want people to take that commitment seriously," she says.

Many years of study and practice have contributed to Dr. Coggin's knowledge of wolves and wolf hybrids. The 1978 graduate of Auburn University's School of Veterinary Medicine began with a malamute— a sled dog from northern North America—which she bred to a wolf hybrid.

"I chose a malamute because it is the only dog that is **Canis Lupus**, the same genus and species as the wolf," explains Dr. Coggin. "My male wolf, Saiga, is a pure strain Alaska grey wolf—**Canis Lupus, Pambicelus**. I chose **Pambicelus** because they are large and the most easily adaptable to people."

Because the wolves and wolf hybrids in North Carolina and Tennessee are so interrelated, Dr. Coggin chose to get her male from Minnesota.

"His genes have never been seen around here. I bought Saiga from Gabe Davidson who runs a fur farm in Minnesota," she says. "I drove to Minnesota and picked him up when he was 18 days of age.

"He lived with me, and I took him everywhere. I took him up to the Highland Games on Grandfather Mountain to acclimate him to people. I wanted him to have an intensive introduction to people when he was young so I could handle him as he grew older.

"He used to love children and would orient to them whenever they were around, but as he grew older I had to keep him up. He started seeking the woods and wandering. It's not that I fear he would attack people, but wolves range for miles and miles to hunt. I worried about people's dogs and livestock," she explains.

The full-grown wolf now weighs 200 pounds, and Dr. Coggins no longer feels completely secure with Saiga.

"When I'm with him, I'm always aware where I am, where he is, and where the gate is. When he came to sexual maturity he tried to add me to his pack. When I'd try to leave the pen he'd grab me with his teeth and pull me back in," she says.

The two females in Dr. Coggin's breeding program are Ootek, a 7/16 eastern timber wolf, and Keyif, a 3/8 Arctic/buffalo wolf. Both females are malamute hybrids.

Keyif lives in the pen with Saiga as his lifelong mate. Ootek lives in an adjacent cage, for the male will allow only the one female who formed his initial pack to be with him.

"He will accept Ootek only when she is in heat. As soon as she is bred, I have to take her out. When Saiga is breeding, he is positively wild, a raving maniac I can't do anything with," Dr. Coggin says.

The hybrid cubs are neither dog nor wolf, but a combination of both.

"They're just pussycats, especially the females. There's such a difference between a pure wolf and a hybrid; even a 29/32 wolf is significantly tamer than a pure wolf. A pure wolf is too bold for anyone to keep as a house pet," she says.

"People who buy the hybrids need to provide a family environment. As pets, they're not good guard dogs. They're too quiet. Wolves are bred to be quiet and stalk prey, which is not what you want from a guard dog.

"Physiologically, hybrids are different from dogs. Their hearts sound different, and they mature much more quickly. By three weeks of age, they're just all over the place, and it's time to get them out. I want them to bond with their owner, not me, for bonding is extremely important," Dr. Coggin says.

While both North Carolina and Tennessee have laws regulating the keeping of wolves, and both require a permit, wolf hybrids occupy a gray area, escaping regulation. Wildlife officials in both states advise caution when dealing with such animals.

Although Dr. Coggin feels confident her hybrids will make good pets, she warns that the breeding of a wolf to a dog should never be attempted.

"My female hybrids were born out of Gordon Smith's breeding program in Iowa. He's genetically culled his hybrids for 30 years until he now has a blended genetic line. Straight wolf-to-dog crosses are temperamentally unstable and considered taboo to breeders," she says.

Thanks to the efforts of such breeders as Gordon Smith and Barbara Coggin, the haunting "O-ooh!" of wolves echoes across the land again. However, today it may come from your neighbor's patio rather than from a thick forest or a projecting mountain rock.

Saiga

WOODFIELD INN

FLAT ROCK, N.C.—History, natural beauty, the arts, fine cuisine and simple relaxation—people go on vacation to seek one or more of these goals. The Woodfield Inn, a 136-year-old country hostelry, provides more than a taste of each.

First planned in 1847 and open for business five years later, the Inn from the beginning has offered more than one would expect. From the "Flat Rock Rocker," a specially made rocking chair that is guaranteed not to creep and not to creak, to the "Lemon Julep" created from lemon trees improbably grown in this cool mountain climate by Squire Farmer, builder and early proprietor, special comforts have awaited the visitors.

While the Flat Rock Rockers still sit on the wide verandas and the Lemon Juleps still cool the palates of weary travelers, other vestiges of the past speak more about the hotel's history.

During the Civil War, a secret storage compartment hidden in the floor of a second story bedroom concealed the gold and valuables of area residents as well as guests of the hotel. This compartment can still be found under the rug, which Jeane Smith, manager of the Woodfield Inn, will be glad to lift.

"The history of the hotel draws many visitors and captures the interest of some who didn't know about it before coming," says Mrs. Smith. "Everything about the Inn speaks of the past."

Wandering the grounds after lunching, Janet Traphagen of nearby Hendersonville, North Carolina, said, "This is a very interesting place, especially the history of it—the carpetbaggers and the soldiers and the trapdoor in the floor."

Confederate soldiers stayed at the Inn to protect it and the surrounding community from renegades that terrorized much of the mountain territories during the late stages of the war. A picture of Captain Morris who led the troops hangs on a foyer wall.

The building itself is an historical artifact and has been named "Inn of the South" by the National Register of Historic Places.

Heading the continuing restoration of the Inn is C. A. Smith, Jeane's husband, who is much impressed by the original construction.

"These 2×4s are real 2×4s." he said, referring to the wall studs. "They're rough cut from heart of pine. I have to drill a hole to put a nail in them. And the smell of pine is just like you cut it yesterday."

He's also happy to show you the hundred-foot well, hand dug by slaves to provide water to the original boarders, and to point out the old root cellar that he's planning to reroof.

Exterior

The natural beauty that first attracted summer visitors over a century ago remains as enchanting as ever. The flower beds and huge old pines, the shrubs and singing birds are as attractive as the historic old buiding.

"It's lovely here. A beautiful place," said Jane Vogan of Rochester, New York, as she walked about the front garden.

And the beauty does not stop with the building and the grounds, filling the Inn are prints and paintings and other objets d'art, as well as hand-crafted coverlets in the Victorian period decorated bedrooms.

One space of wall in the living room holds four original Hogarth prints from the *MARRIAGE À LA MODE* series, a taste of the 18th century that seems right at home in this time capsule of an inn.

On the next wall is a well-crammed bookcase, containing no new best sellers, but many past ones, including a much-read collection of Dickens.

The snug bedrooms with fireplaces and French doors leading to the cool verandas with the rocking chairs and plenty of fresh air encourage reading.

"None of the rooms have televisions except the suite. At one time every room had them, and phones too, but everyone thought they were out of place, so we took them out," says Mrs. Smith.

Other art interests are the nearby Flat Rock Theatre with professional entertainment throughout the summer and the Carl Sandburg Estate, the last home of the famous poet. Guests often walk to these places, which are only a few blocks away.

Such strolls help to build a hearty appetite to bring to the Inn's tables. From its opening the Inn has been famous for abundant and delicious cuisine, and today's chefs continue the tradition.

"We've just hired two chefs who are just great," says Ms. Smith. "The response of the guests has been tremendous."

A glance through the guest book confirms her enthusiasm. Among the tributes to the atmosphere and natural beauty are references to specific meals such as the trout and the prime rib.

And a visit to the dining room ends any doubts. Dinner begins with a basket of hot rolls, bread, or corn muffins and a huge relish platter with fresh vegetables, cheese, dips, and pickled snacks. Entrees such as mountain trout almondine and herb-fried chicken are served with skillfully cooked vegetables.

Guests are encouraged to bring their own wine or liquor to complement the meals. The famous Lemon Julep demands a jigger of whiskey to be complete; a pitcher on the porch may be all the entertainment you want.

The lack of hustle and bustle may be the Woodfield Inn's greatest

Living Room

attraction. Few places today encourage you to simply sit and relax—the Inn with its broad verandas, cool breezes, and acres of green to insulate you from even the two lane road that passes by demands that you accept its leisurely pace.

Jim and Tommie Morris now of Morrow, Georgia, an Atlanta suburb, were found rocking on the second story veranda.

Mrs. Morris, who was born and raised in Roan Mountain, Tennessee, was glad to be back in the mountains.

"We've never been here before, but we love it. It's such a change from the city," she said. Their major decision of the evening was whether to walk or drive to the Carl Sandburg Home before dining.

There are certain places that seem imbued with the spirit of the past, and the Woodfield Inn is one of these. "These walls talk to me," said Carl Sandburg when he first entered the Inn, and that feeling is shared by all who find themselves stepping from the hurly-burly of late 20th century civilization into the cool calmness of this 19th century country inn.

The Woodfield Inn is located on Highway 25 South, 2½ miles from Hendersonville, North Carolina, and 1½ miles from Interstate 26. For information write Box 98, Flat Rock, NC 28731 or call 704/693-6016.

BLACKSMITH

Under a spreading chestnut-tree
The village smithy stands;
The smith, a mighty man is he,
With large and sinewy hands;
And the muscles of his brawny arms
Are strong as iron bands.

—Henry Wadsworth Longfellow

BULADEAN, N. C.—Much has changed since Longfellow wrote his enduring poem almost 150 years ago. The forge is no longer a center of town life, and large chestnut trees have disappeared, the victims of blight.

However, still today "large and sinewy hands" can be found to forge a horseshoe, and "brawny arms" to nail it to the horse's hoof.

Cut from the same cloth as Longfellow's exemplary hero is Vernon Buchanan, who travels winding mountain roads seeing that today's horses are shod as carefully as yesterday's.

"Most people call me a horse-shoer. The word 'farrier' is not used much up here, but it would be the proper term I suppose," says Buchanan, who has practiced his trade, art, skill—"It's probably all three"—for more than 25 years.

"I used to travel from Beckley, West Virginia, to Knoxville, Tennessee, to Hickory, North Carolina, shoeing horses. Today I stick pretty much to Mitchell, Yancey, Avery, McDowell, and Madison counties in North Carolina," Buchanan says.

Because of the size of his territory, Buchanan drives his pickup truck from farm to farm, spending long, hot days with the horses and horsemen who rely on his expertise.

"I've got more than I can do. I'm not complaining, but sometimes I'm hesitant to answer the phone," he says.

While the smaller horseshoes can be bought ready-made for cold shoeing, the larger shoes must be forged by hand, hot-shoeing.

"You can put them to whatever hardness you want while you're forging. You can temper them to be soft or harder, whatever you want. It depends on how it'll be used," Buchanan says.

A picture of this modern blacksmith could well be used to illustrate Longfellow's poem. In his split apron, wielding tools that haven't changed in hundreds of years, and grasping the horse's hoof in his strong hands, Buchanan works with sweat glistening on his brow and without modern technology.

The basis of his work is the age-old relationship of man and horse.

"You've just got to get along with them. A horse can hurt you, not out of meanness but just because they're so big and so strong," Buchanan says.

"Patience has a lot to do with it. You've got to take the time that it takes for the horse, and each is different.

"Also, you can't be afraid of the horse. I'm not afraid of them, but I've got respect for horses," he says.

Gaining expertise in his work has been a lifelong process for Buchanan.

"I had horses when I was a kid. They had to have shoes, so I learned to do my own, and kinda branched out from there, got bigger and bigger.

"I spend a lot of time up in the Amish part of Ohio. I make two or three trips a year," he says. "You'll see a fellow out in a field. He'll have his hitch of six or eight horses, and his wife will have her hitch. The women can work them just as well as the men.

"The Amish have a lot bigger horses; the bigger they are, the better they like them," Buchanan explains. "Those long strides cover the field that much faster. In these mountains, a smaller horse will get over the hills a lot better than a big one, so we have smaller horses here.

"On Amish farms you hardly ever see a shoe on their work horses, but in this part there's so many rocks, and the ground's so rough, it breaks their feet up if they don't have shoes," he says. "Also, you get better traction with shoes."

Horses are plentiful in the mountain counties, where many farmers still use horse power to work their land. Getting horses shod correctly is important to these men who tend steep plots.

"There's a lot of people that can put a shoe on, but having the hoof trimmed just right and having the shoe fit just right are important," Buchanan says. "If it's not right, the shoe will come off.

"I'd shoe your horse just like I do mine, and I want mine to be shod the very best," he says.

With about 25 horses and mules of his own, Buchanan is never far from the creatures that have formed the framework for his life since he was a boy.

His knowledge and rapport with the beasts is evident from the time he lays a gentling hand on one until he rasps smooth the hoof around the last shoe.

Each hoof is carefully cleaned out, nipped down, and shaved smooth

Vernon Buchanan

and level before the shoe is fit. Each shoe is carefully shaped, flattened, and placed before a nail is touched. Each nail is set with extra care before being nailed in place.

"It's how far inside the hoof you get that's important," Buchanan says. "Too far, they'll definitely go lame, and you can set up tetanus. Usually as soon as it sets the hoof down, you can tell if it's bothering the horse."

When the horse is shod, Buchanan carefully cleans and wraps his files, then stows his equipment in the wooden cradle that travels with him.

While his tools are simple, his skills are not. Whether he's handling the large beasts in a way that soothes rather than annoys, snatching a horsefly from a quivering flank before the insect bites, or clinching the nails tight, the work is done well.

Longfellow's stalwart example of 150 years ago would be proud of his southern progeny, Vernon Buchanan, whose ways reflect the same dedication and care that made the village blacksmith a byword for reliability and industry.

RAISING SHEEP

BAKERSVILLE, N.C.—Times are hard for farmers.

High land costs (especially in the summer tourist territories of the mountains), lowered tobacco allotments with increased costs, heavy interest rates and increased worldwide competition have made farming a hobby or a second job for most of those living on what were productive farms for generations into the past.

Mitchell County, North Carolina, has suffered as much as most rural areas; however, today, renewed interest in an age-old food source raises hope in many that better times lie ahead.

Sheep, those biblical animals, are making a comeback in the mountains of Western North Carolina.

Only a generation ago, in the 1950s and '60s, thousands of sheep were raised in the coves and on the hillsides of Mitchell County. By 1970 less than a handful remained. An entire industry had been destroyed by dogs, one or two of which can kill 75 to 100 head of sheep in a single night.

As Gary Hyatt, North Carolina agricultural extension specialist, explained, "People gave up on the sheep because of the dogs. When attacked, the sheep run wildly as long as they can, then just fall over and quit."

However, with new techniques of electric fencing, Hyatt believes there is a good chance that raising sheep will provide an important addition to local farmers' incomes.

Hyatt explained that most pasture land in the county is not used. With more than 18,000 acres of pasture, Mitchell County farmers raise only about 2,000 head of cattle.

Left idle, much of the land used for farming earlier in the century is reverting to woodland. One acre can sustain three to five sheep, as opposed to only one-and-a-half cows. The potential for profitable sheep raising is obvious.

Grazing the sheep year-round means inexpensive feed which yields valuable meat and wool. Sheep do not ruin their grazing grounds, despite the claims of cattlemen in old western movies; although they do clip the grass more closely than cows and must be rotated from pasture to pasture.

With the encouragement of the Agricultural Extension Service, about 10 farms in Mitchell County are experimenting with sheep. Hyatt hopes that the success of these ventures will persuade more farmers to diversify by adding sheep raising to their programs.

Mitchell County sheep herd

At Jim and Delores Miller's farm, their first year's experiment with sheep has impressed them both favorably.

"We had them when I was a boy," said Jim Miller, explaining why he chose to try raising the wooly animals, "and I liked them then. They are a lot better than cattle, not as much trouble."

When asked about the dog problem, he said that he hadn't had any trouble yet after almost a year in the business and that for $36 his flock of 60 sheep was fully insured for a year. Even if the dogs attacked, he would lose nothing.

The Millers expect to recover their investment with the marketing of their first year's lambs. Less than 12 months from when he got his flock, he has wool to sell, as well as the lambs.

The return from the sale of these first offspring of his ewes should cover the cost of the flock itself. His Suffolk and Cheviot sheep couldn't please him more.

Lamb prices are high because bad weather the past few years has reduced flocks across the country. The drought in Texas, as well as other areas, combined with the severe winters to produce shortages of marketable lambs.

When asked about the disadvantages, all Hyatt or the Millers could think of was the danger from dogs and problems with parasites, particularly worms. So far the dogs have not appeared, and with regular care, the parasites are easily controlled.

"I like them," said Delores Miller enthusiastically. "Although we still have cattle, the sheep are easier to take care of." Both she and her husband join Hyatt in readily recommending the addition of sheep to a farm's livestock.

For those interested in sheep raising, Hyatt is available to provide information and aid. He sends a newsletter, checks on facilities, and helps get the farmer started with his flock. Hyatt even helps with shearing the wool.

"My help's supposed to be mainly educational," he laughed, "but most of the time I end up shearing." Everyone agreed that shearing can be learned but it's hard on the back.

These changing times may be bringing back an ancient art to the mountains. Soon those weed-filled pastures climbing into steep mountain coves may be filled with a more profitable crop—the white, wooly sheep.

It was a hot Thursday evening, too hot to be thinking about wool. However, Buster Honeycutt was thinking about just that commodity.

It was sheep shearing time on his farm.

Thirty years ago many farmers in Western North Carolina would have been thinking about the same thing; ten years ago practically no one had wool on his mind. In the 1950s and early '60s over 4,000 of the wooly animals thrived in the lush mountain pastures, but wild dogs destroyed the entire industry.

Recently the Extension Office decided to try again.

"About three years ago we really got going; before that there might have been 30 or 40 head at most," said Gary Hyatt, sheep specialist of the Mitchell County Agricultural Extension Office. "It's close to 400 ewes in the county now, I'd guess."

According to Hyatt, two years ago there were less than 10 farmers experimenting with sheep with the Extension Office; today there are between 20 and 25. And there appears no end to such growth in the near future.

Good prices, low expense, and electric fencing have been responsible for the renewed success of the sheep in the mountains.

"For the last nine weeks lambs have brought over 90 cents a pound in Virginia," said Hyatt. "A choice grade lamb weighs over 95 pounds and under 125. The demand is strong, and by the end of June we'll have some pretty good loads to sell up there."

The cost of ewes that have been bred is presently about $100. A healthy ewe can produce abundant offspring over the years.

"Some of them go 20 years; some only 5 or 6. The average is 7 to 10 years of breeding. Ewes average 1.5 lambs a year," said Hyatt, letting the numbers speak for themselves.

While sheep need shelter for lambing, tobacco barns fill that need well. Lambing time comes after the tobacco has been cured and sold, and shearing is done in the late spring while tobacco is in the beds or has just been set.

"I had to build the lambing pens, but my tobacco barn was already here," said Honeycutt, who bought his first ewes this past November.

"In the winter I fed the ewes 16% dairy feed and hay. They're on pasture now," he added.

Mitchell County has many acres of pasture land that have been going back to woodland through lying idle over the past few decades.

Electric fencing has saved the sheep from dogs, two of which can kill a hundred sheep in one night, explained Honeycutt. So far he has had no trouble with dogs.

In fact, the entire county has done well against the animals that destroyed the industry a generation ago.

"Me, I'm the only one who has lost any. I lost 14 last winter to a

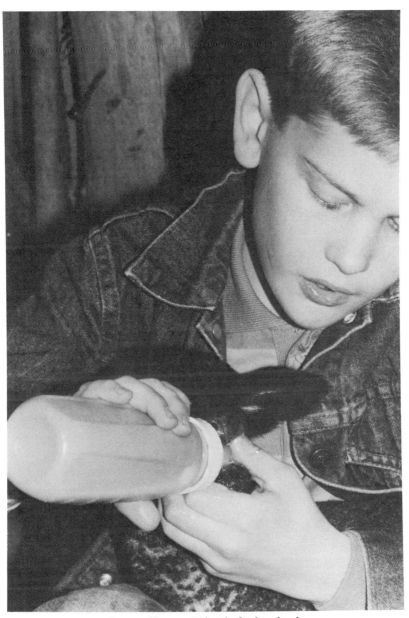

Jeremy Honeycutt bottle feeds a lamb

pack of wild dogs," said Hyatt sheepishly. "And I didn't even have insurance. I told everybody else to get it but didn't myself."

An added bonus in the sheep business is the sale of wool, although the money may not seem much for the work to the novice shearer.

"We have a wool pool in Asheville that pays 63 cents a pound for the wool," said Hyatt. "We get about 6 to 8 pounds of wool per sheep; however, one county ram had 18 pounds of wool from one year's growth."

Shearing is not easy for beginners, although with the experience gained over the past few years Hyatt makes it look not too difficult.

After watching attentively for several sheep, Honeycutt tried his hand with the electric clippers. After wrestling with the ewe for a bit, he clipped off some clumps and drew some blood, but then slid along its flank in a long, smooth shear.

"We're trying to get as much wool off as we can and leave as much sheep there as we can," said Hyatt with a laugh.

Honeycutt's son, Jeremy, paid close attention to the whole process and even tried a clip or two. His generation will have the knowledge that was lost along with the sheep.

Spring shearing will once again be an annual mountain ritual.

BRINEGAR CABIN

BLUE RIDGE PARKWAY—Today with the Blue Ridge Parkway providing easy travel along the steep ridges, it is difficult to imagine the isolation and hardships faced by mountain farmers at the turn of the century. However, the Brinegar Cabin farmsite at milepost 238.5 evokes much of that life.

While the old farmstead was purchased in two tracts in 1935 and 1937 by the National Park Service and for years has been a popular site, recent studies directed by Dr. Barry Buxton, Executive Director of the Appalachian Consortium, have developed the historical and personal perspectives of the once thriving homestead.

Buxton's research has established that the cabin was built by Martin Brinegar and his wife Caroline during the 1880s. The couple raised their family in an independent lifestyle typical of isolated mountain farmers of the period.

Crops such as buckwheat, rye, oats, corn, squash, beans, tomatoes, potatoes and pumpkins were grown on the cleared land, while horses, cows, goats, hogs and poultry grazed on the pastures and fattened on the forest mast. An orchard of antique variety apples also contributed to the Brinegars' abundant life.

Cash money came from Martin's work as a cobbler.

"A pair of Uncle Martin's shoes usually lasted us two years because we went barefoot back then in the summertime," said neighbor Sherman Caudill. "He'd come over to our place and say 'hold that foot up' and he'd pick your foot up and rub the shoe and check it for wear. He was so proud of them shoes."

Grandson Kyle Brinegar recalls that it took Martin about two weeks to make a pair of shoes that cost around a dollar, depending on size.

Wife Caroline contributed to the family's cash by weaving linsey-woolsey cloth on the four-poster hand loom received as a wedding present. An almost 200-year-old loom and a handcrafted working reproduction stand in the cabin today.

Although the barn was torn down to make way for the road construction, the original cabin, granary, and spring house stand firmly on the site now to give visitors a glimpse into the past of Southern Appalachia.

"Today everyone has really enjoyed it," said Ranger Dorothy Cook on a recent Saturday morning. "I opened an hour ago at 9 and already 23 people have come through."

"Everybody always finds the sleeping loft fascinating. They had so much room up there. And it's amazing how many kids know that this is actually a working loom. Most people get their ideas about cabins from *LITTLE HOUSE ON THE PRAIRIE*, and they didn't have a loom," said Cook.

Many of the visitors hike down from nearby Doughton Park which has a campground and a variety of trails. Others make a special trip to the Parkway just to visit and revisit the farmsite, while some simply see the signs and stop in.

During the summer Brinegar Cabin is open from 9 a.m. to 5 p.m. on Saturdays and Sundays. Other times the site can be visited but the buildings are closed.

"We came up to see the insides of the cabin and other buildings," said Felton Bollinger from Waxhaw, North Carolina. "We were here six months ago and it had just closed, so we were curious to see what we'd missed."

"We will have people on weekends doing exhibitions of basketry, weaving, woodworking, mountain music and other crafts to complement the site," said Cook.

The simple beauty of the buildings is reason enough to add to the enjoyment of a drive on the Parkway with a stop at the Brinegar Cabin. Also, the information gathered by researchers makes the stop an educational one.

"The Brinegar Cabin, and the lives of Martin and Caroline Brinegar, are representative of folk culture among Highland families around the turn of the century. From their fierce individualism to the subsistence farming and religious fundamentalism they practiced, their lives paralleled the day to day lifestyle of most of their neighbors," wrote Barry Buxton in his study.

Brinegar Cabin

LINVILLE CAVERNS

LINVILLE CAVERNS, N.C.—A natural retreat from the wilting heat of summer lies deep under Humpback Mountain just off the Blue Ridge Parkway.

At a consistent 52 degrees throughout the year, Linville Caverns offer both a pleasant respite from outside extremes and beautiful natural formations to delight the eye.

Although they were officially discovered about one hundred years ago, North Carolina's only known, large limestone caverns have an ancient natural history.

A half billion years ago the area was under the sea. The millions of sea creatures and plants secreted calcium carbonate, a lime-like material, that accumulated, becoming hundreds of feet thick, then hardening into a rock layer known as Shady Dolomite.

Groundwater has dissolved this material, forming the caverns, a process that continues today.

"The original water-filled solution cavities must have come into existence sometime after Appalachian Mountain building forces elevated the Shady Dolomite above sea level. This was somewhere in the neighborhood of 230 million years ago. Because the last major cycle of erosion began approximately 30 million years ago, it is possible that the original cavities of Linville Caverns were born at that time," writes Henry S. Brown in his pamphlet **Linville Caverns Through the Ages: The Geological Story**.

While man's role in the history of the caverns is of course much more recent, there is still uncertainty about how long their existence has been known.

"In the late 1880s a man fishing noticed trout going out of the mountain. He followed the stream through a hole and found the caverns," says Everett Carpenter, one of the guides who lead the tours and explain the wonders of Linville Caverns.

"The only dry spot in the caverns then was a sandbar. On the sandbar were an old campfire and a cobbler's bench. Civil War deserters from both sides hid in the caverns, and these were the only remains," he adds, pointing to the still visible sandbar.

"I believe that the people in the area knew about the caverns for years, and you couldn't keep a spot like this secret from the Indians, but the official discoverer was H. E Colton from eastern North Carolina and his guide Dave Franklin," says Carpenter.

As you walk through the caverns, the guides provide such information while they point out the more interesting features and explain the natural processes that have created them.

One such feature is the Ballroom, a 60 foot by 20 foot area with a five foot ceiling.

"It was called the Ballroom because the floor was smooth enough to dance on. At least it was before they fell through. The floor was only a quarter inch thick," says Everett.

"The Ballroom is a solution cavity. That means that water seeped through a crack; it was slightly acidic and dissolved the limestone," he adds.

Throughout the caverns are stalactite and stalagmite formations created by the dripping mineral-laden water. The Frozen Waterfall, the Altar, the Monster's Hands, the Shepherd, and many other fancifully named water-made creations fill the caverns.

Linville Caverns were first commercialized in 1937 by John Quincy Gilkey from nearby Marion, North Carolina. Since that time many thousands of tourists have travelled through them.

The caverns are a popular destination for school field trips, as well as for tourists.

"We get bus loads from West Virginia, South Carolina, Tennessee, Virginia, and from North Carolina," says Tina Nanney, public relations director. "March through May we're always busy with schools."

"In the winter most of our traffic comes from skiers. The ski slopes are just above us. In the summer and fall mostly we get tourists here to see the mountains. Many come especially to visit the caverns," she says.

One family to tour Linville Caverns recently was the Millers. Jim and Judy Miller and their four girls drove up from Clayton, Georgia, to camp nearby.

"I'd been in the caverns when I was little and I wanted to come back and show my girls," said Mrs. Miller. "The girls loved it. I'm sure we'll be coming back."

Children seem especially fascinated by the eerie, underground world of the caverns. Their unabashed "Ooohs," and "Ahhs," punctuate the tour.

Linville Caverns are open the year around, except for Christmas and Thanksgiving. Each morning the doors open at 9:00, and from June 1 through Labor Day they close at 6:00 p.m., April, May, September and October they close at 5:00, and the rest of the year at 4:00 p.m..

Admission is $1.50 for children 5 through 11 and $3.00 for those 12 and up. Special rates are available to large groups.

To find Linville Caverns, drive south on Highway 221 four miles past the Blue Ridge Parkway between Linville and Marion, North Carolina.

It's a cool way to spend a summer day.

One of the many cave formations with colorful nicknames; this one is "The Bat."

ELK FALLS

ELK PARK, N.C.—The Elk River is one of the many things that bind together North Carolina and Tennessee. It is a thread stitching one state to the other.

An outstanding feature of this river is the Elk Falls, lying just inside the North Carolina border. In an explosion of mist and thunder, the Elk plunges over a steep granite cliff into a large basin carved over the millenia.

For many years local residents have sought the cool beauty of Elk Falls for summertime relaxation and relief from the heat. Even when a cool morning makes the water too frigid for enjoyment, the sight and sound of the Falls reward a visit.

In the early days of this century, Shepherd M. Dugger, "The Bard of Ottaray," made the area an important part of his short story, "John Kite's Log-Rolling."

He opens the story with the following description:

"In the northwest corner of Avery County, Elk Creek leaps into Tennessee, down over great ledges of granite. Chief of these is the Falls of Elk, thundering in its foam and spray like the thunder in the clouds."

In the 1950s, Paul Hughes Neal in his novel **Along These Trails** had the Falls teach his young hero several lessons about himself and his relationships with others.

First he learns courage and self-confidence when he faces "the ninety-foot drop of solid gray rock" into "the great pool at the base, clear as glass and under it a solid granite bottom."

"We raced to the edge and I bent my knees and arched my back and sailed out and down into the great clear pool. When we climbed out, Big Will held out his hand. 'Nice going, Kid. I'm proud of you.'"

Next he learns the price of self-respect when he weighs the ethics of entertaining the summer people by diving over the Falls for silver dollars they throw to the local youths.

"When I was teaching at Lees-McRae College in the 1950s, my students did tell me that such things happened in the summer. The local teenage boys dove for silver dollars tossed by the tourists," said Neal recently.

Over the years, such heroics have cost the lives of several people. As Neal wrote in his book, "There was white water boiling at the base of the Falls. I had to go beyond that. There was a ledge that had to be cleared."

"Every summer it seems someone is killed or seriously hurt at the

Blanche Joslin at Elk Falls

Falls. Some try diving in instead of jumping, and there are large rocks just four feet under the surface in places,'' said Paul Medynski, owner of Mountain Image, a Banner Elk photo-processing business.

With care, such hazards can be avoided. The U.S. Forest Service maintains a recreation area at the site, with picnic tables, fences around the dangerous upper falls, and steps leading to the basin.

The solid rock of the basin provides a safe margin for play or swimming. Leave the leaping to fictional heroes.

The simple pleasure of seeing the white curtain flowing, hearing the booming thunder, and feeling the vibration and the cool mist of the Falls is attraction enough for most people. The easy access by stairs makes maneuvering around the site simple.

The Appalachian Trail Commission is considering moving the Trail itself so that hikers on the Georgia-to-Maine path will experience the wonders of Elk Falls.

"Where the Trail is now is pleasant, but the river is spectacular. We feel that moving the trail along the river would be a definite improvement. It would add a couple of miles and have at least a mile along the Elk River,'' said Morgan Sommerville a spokesman for the ATC.

"We would like to do it, but we are only in the preliminary stages of consideration now,'' he said.

A threat to the scenic beauty of the site is a proposed clearcut by the Pisgah Forest of the Forest Service. The Forest Service's environmental impact statement estimates that approximately 50% of the clearcut will be visible from the waterfalls.

Elk Falls can be reached by traveling 19E from Roan Mountain, Tennessee, to cross the state line at Elk Park, North Carolina. Turn left just opposite the Sunset Market in Elk Park, then take another left onto state road 1305. Follow beside the river; after the road turns to gravel you will pass the Forest Service sign just before the Falls.

Dylan and Blanche at base of falls.

Bumblebee on a Roan Mountain Rhododendron.

ROAN MOUNTAIN
RHODODENDRON FESTIVAL

ROAN MOUNTAIN, N.C.—As the year circles into summer, thousands converge on Roan Mountain to celebrate the annual miracle of the blossoming of the rhododendron gardens.

This rich profusion of purple-red flowers rewards all who make the journey to this 6,286-foot bald and forms the focus for the Rhododendron Festivals of Bakersville, North Carolina, and Roan Mountain, Tennessee.

While official festivals have been held here for over 40 years, the summer celebration has flourished for many more years than that.

One of the world's oldest mountains, the Roan has supported life for over 250 million years, as have many of the Southern Appalachians' higher peaks. Naturalist-writer Donald Culross Peattie believes that the first flowering plants above the rank of conifers originated in these mountains some 95 million years ago.

Lying beyond the reach of the great ice sheets of the glacial period, this area preserved some of the oldest types of plants and thus maintains the most varied flora in the world. These ancient flowers find relatives in such far-off places as China, Japan, Nepal, and Tibet.

Long before the first white man reached America's shores, Indians had visited the Roan and lived in the sheltered coves on the mountain's sides. Today, along the swift-running mountain streams, Indian artifacts can still be found.

While the bald summit of the Roan experiences winters too harsh for comfortable habitation, during the summer months the Indians gathered for celebration and, occasionally, confrontation on the broad meadows grazed by large herds of elk and buffalo.

According to a legend recounted by the late C. Rex Peake, a longtime resident and protector of the Roan, one June the Cherokees, the mountain Indians, met the Catawbas, a Piedmont tribe, on Roan Mountain in a pitched battle. The Catawba braves suffered tremendous losses.

Spilling onto the mountain, the blood of these Indians blossomed as flowers on the rhododendron, giving the Catawba Rhododendron its name.

With the coming of the white man, interest developed in the unusual flora of this high mountain bald. From the late 18th century through today, a caravan of botanists and naturalists has visited the Roan to explore, catalog, and collect.

In August 1794, Andre Michaux, a renowned French botanist, first traveled the wilderness roads to reach the then-isolated Roan after several years of exploration to the south. He returned in May 1795, to complete his study of the wonders of the mountain.

In 1799, a colleague who had traveled with Michaux during his first journey into the more southern mountains in 1787, Scottish naturalist John Fraser, discovered and collected on the Roan the rhododendron that is celebrated annually today.

A "new" plant to the botanists of the day, the **Rhododendron Catawbiense** created tremendous interest among collectors and gardeners, who have developed many different hybrids from this mountain beauty.

Following these two explorer-botanists, in the early decades of the 19th century came John Lyon, the Rev. M. A. Curtis, and Thomas Nuttall, who collected specimens from the Roan to send to gardens throughout the United States and Europe, as well as continuing to discover new plants.

In 1835, Elisha Mitchell, the geographer who gave his name and life to Mt. Mitchell, climbed the Roan to pursue his studies of the North Carolina mountains. His description captures well the mountain's unique quality.

"It is the most beautiful and will best repay the labor of ascending it of all our high mountains. With the exception of rocks looking like the ruins of an old castle near its southwestern extremity, the top of Roan may be described as a vast meadow without a tree to obstruct a prospect, where a person may gallop his horse for a mile or two, with Carolina at his feet on one side and Tennessee on the other, and a green ocean of mountains raised into tremendous billows immediately about him.

"It is the elysium of the Southern Botanist, as a number of plants are found growing in this cold and humid atmosphere which are not seen again until we have gone hundreds of miles further north."

Six years later, in early July, Asa Gray, a Harvard professor and botanist, made his first ascent of the Roan. His preoccupation with the view was no different from that of today's visitors.

"It was just sunset when we reached the bald and grassy summit of this noble mountain, and after enjoying for a moment the magnificent view it affords, had barely time to prepare our encampment between two dense clumps of **Rhododendron Catawbiense**," he wrote.

One of the Roan's most famous plants, the Roan Lily or Gray's Lily, was named for Asa Gray and continues to attract botanists today.

As access to the mountains became easier, more and more naturalists made the journey to the Roan. This list stretches to this day, with the Roan massif continuously under study as cessation of grazing has allowed a natural succession of woody shrubs and trees to occur.

Joining the scientists in the late 19th century were many tourists. In 1877 Gen. J. T. Wilder built a 20-room log inn on the summit of the Roan, and eight years later he added a 166-room frame building called the Cloudland Hotel.

The East Tennessee and Western North Carolina Railroad, nicknamed the "Tweetsie," brought guests to the foot of the steep climb to the mountain, where carriages then carried them up to the hotel.

Advertisements for the Cloudland Hotel in 1885-86 invited tourists to "Come up out of the sultry plain to the 'Land of the Sky,' magnificent views above the clouds where rivers are born, a most extended prospect of 50,000 square miles in six different states, one hundred mountain tops over 4,000 feet high in sight."

Local musicians entertained the guests, while other residents went to the hotel for entertainment and refreshments, some of which were supplied by local moonshiners. Such were the origins of the celebrations that have grown into today's Rhododendron Festivals.

Shortly after the turn of the century, the Cloudland Hotel closed, and the stands of Fraser fir were sold to timber companies. Also, the root stock of the rhododendron was sold to nurseries, which hauled them off the mountain, leaving a devastated landscape.

The mountain was largely denuded in this last effort to wring money from its summit.

"The best were taken," says Bob Carey of the U.S. Forest Service's Toecane District Office. "They left only some poor, straggling stock. What we have now has grown out from these."

The magnificent gardens that grace the Roan today owe little to man's care. Weathering both abuse and exploitation, the mountain's millenia-old strength residing in its rich soil flourishes forth the glowing rhododendron blossoms that bring visitors from all over the planet.

To keep the rhododendron the dominant plant in the gardens, the Forest Service has begun to remove the spruce and fir trees that would overshadow the flowering bushes in the natural succession as the trees encroach on the bald.

In addition to maintaining the gardens, the Forest Service keeps the roads and trails suitable for the visitors. The summer celebrants in the distant past were few compared to the thousands that flock to the mountain now.

"The only problems we have are people picking the flowers and parking along the road rather than in the parking lots," says Carey. "There are many plants, including rare ones, that get mashed down by careless parking."

Under the full moon on the summer solstice, both Tennessee and North Carolina celebrate the renewal of the gardens. Everyone is invited to join.

Morning dew on Catawba Rhododendron.

Gray's Lily Blossom

GRAY'S LILY

ROAN MOUNTAIN—For most people, Roan Mountain means the rhododendrons and the festivals that celebrate the world famous gardens. However, for many local mountain folks and flower-loving aficionados, the blossoming of the rhododendrons is merely a brilliant interlude in the year-round wonder of the massif, and a prelude to the appearance of the gem-like Roan Lily or Gray's Lily (**Lilium Grayi**). In many ways this rare flower symbolizes the concerns of those who live upon the mountain and those who want to preserve the natural beauty of the balds.

In the Bakersville Library a manual on wildflowers identifies this flower as the Orange Bell Lily. A local patron has indignantly scratched out this designation to write in, in indelible ink, Roan Lily or Gray's Lily.

Mountain folks have their pride, and this flower is part of it.

Early in July the slender but strong stalks with ranked whorls of green leaves send forth the deep orange-red blossoms that glow like candle flames on the massif.

The Gray's Lily was first discovered on Roan Mountain in the 19th century, but over the years since, populations have been found in some other places in North Carolina, Tennessee, and Virginia.

"There are 27 populations throughout the range, but there used to be more than that. Some cannot be found now. Roan Mountain has the largest population," says Nora Murdock, a biologist with the U. S. Fish and Wildlife Service.

Keeping this rare plant is a major concern of many who are involved with the mountain and its ecology, from state governments to local residents.

"In North Carolina, Gray's Lily is listed as Threatened, and in Tennessee it is Endangered," says Ms. Murdock. "It is a candidate for a federal listing as Endangered or Threatened. The information that we have indicates that it should have a federal listing, but more research is necessary."

The lily was first described in 1879 by Sereno Watson, who named it for his mentor, the pioneering American botanist Asa Gray. Gray had first visited the Roan in 1841, and the mountain held a special place in his heart for the rest of his life.

"The Roan is well characterized by Prof. Mitchell as the easiest of access and the most beautiful of all the high mountains of that region," wrote Gray about his first ascent.

"At sunrise we had fine weather and a most extensive view of the surrounding country; in one direction we could count from eight to

A clump of Gray's Lilies

Triple blossom of Gray's Lily plant

twelve successive ranges of the mountains, and nearly all the higher peaks of this whole region were distinctly visible. Soon, however, we were enveloped in a dense fog which continued for several hours, during which we traversed the southwestern summit, and made a list of plants.''

On this list is **Lilium Canadense**, a species of lily that closely resembles **Lilium Grayi**, according to Jim Massey, director of the Herbarium at UNC-Chapel Hill. So Gray may have discovered this plant on his first visit, but failed to distinguish it from its near relative, a mistake the uninformed still make.

Gray returned to the Roan several times in his life, even staying at the Cloudland Hotel with his wife. His protégé and assistant, Sereno Watson, honored Gray by naming the lily after him.

Botanists are still busy on the mountain conducting inventories and monitoring the endangered, rare and sensitive plant species, of which the Roan Lily is one.

"We don't know a lot about it—how it grows, how well it reproduces," says Marjorie Boyer of the North Carolina Plant Conservation Program. "We do know that poaching is definitely a problem."

"It grows out in the open. People see it and say 'Wouldn't it look lovely in my front yard,' but it is not legal to dig it up. The agency gives some permits to people to propagate the plant from seed, but it is strictly regulated. I want to be clear that it is completely illegal to collect plants or to sell plants collected from the wild," she adds.

In addition to poaching, overgrazing and development have destroyed some of the fragile habitats for the Gray's Lily.

"They have been overgrazed, paved over, and built on," says Herbarium director Massey. "And it's such a wonderful plant; it's so showy. When I was up there last year, I noticed people were picking the blossoms off the plants, then just throwing them down as they walked along."

The lily can be seen growing beside the road to the rhododendron gardens for those who don't hike, and along the Appalachian Trail that crosses the balds.

Don't pick the flowers or disturb their habitat; their beauty is reward enough for the trip to the mountain.

FRANK HOLLIFIELD'S CHRISTMAS TREES

LITTLE SWITZERLAND, N.C.—The death of the American small farm has been chronicled in every medium. Yet, as Mark Twain once said, "Reports of my death are greatly exaggerated."

True, the life of the small farmer is not an easy one, for the giant agricultural corporations compete ruthlessly for the consumer's dollar. Errors in judgment and slackness in performance no longer slip by without serious consequences.

Nevertheless, many small farmers manage to coax from the earth a fruitful existence for themselves and their families, while providing quality products for the market and protecting the land that sustains them.

One such farmer is Frank Hollifield, a Christmas tree grower who has been selected as the Mitchell Soil and Water Conservation District Farm Family of the Year.

"A lot of factors go into selection," said Cliff Vinson of the Soil Conservation Service. "We were influenced by the quality of his trees, the fact that he has no erosion problems, and that on his whole farm he's doing a real good job in every aspect of land care and crop production."

"Everytime we come out to his farm we learn something," added Ken Deyton, another SCS employee.

"His attitude is his real strength," Vinson said. "Several times he's told me that he feels that the land is not his, but something he must take care of for those who will follow him. And the way he farms shows that's how he feels."

Farming is not something that Hollifield rushed into. For most of his life he worked in construction. Only in the last six or seven years has he turned to farming full-time.

He slipped into growing trees over a number of years, beginning in 1967.

"I took a step at a time," he recalled. "No one knew then that we'd be able to sell the trees. I had time to learn the business as it developed in this area."

And learn it he did. Today his trees go to wholesalers throughout the Southeast. This year's crop is already sold. In January the buyers come to his Little Switzerland farm and buy the trees to be cut for the following Christmas.

"He doesn't rush his trees," explained Vinson. "He takes his time and does a really good job."

"We harvest from 7 feet and up," said Hollifield, as he walked through his rows of trees. "I try not to cut any 6-foot trees at all."

He pointed to a beautifully tapered, full Fraser fir, saying, "A lot of fellers would have took that tree, or that," he gestured to another one, slightly taller than himself. "But when it gets that size, it will really improve with each year's growth."

Hollifield agrees competition in Christmas tree sales is stiff but relies on the knowledge that quality sells.

"I do see problems in it (overproduction). In fact, there are some difficulties right now," he explained. "But there will always be a market for a quality Fraser."

Like any good farmer, Hollifield feels deeply the cyclical nature of his work. He is sure of the wheel of the seasons and the rotation of his trees.

"Each time we take a tree out, we transplant one back," he said as he strolled through a mixed planting where trees ranged from 2-footers just planted from lineout beds to giants over 20 feet tall.

One of his primary concerns is maintaining the land; he looks down the years to his children and grandchildren, knowing a fertile land will sustain them as it has sustained him.

Instead of blanketing his fields with herbicides to kill grasses and weeds, he uses a mower he's constructed with shields to protect the lower limbs of his trees.

"One of my goals is to get across that a man ought to be considerate using herbicides and pesticides," he stressed.

"If you can leave the grass, erosion is no problem. Grass holds the ground," Hollifield explained. "The soil doesn't wash and your fertilizer holds."

Moving to a large mound of soil covered with thick grass, Hollifield showed how he keeps improving his land.

"Roots and plants are what build your topsoil," he said as he pointed at the cut-away side of the mound which showed the process clearly.

Another soil-saving practice the tree grower employs is to clear land by bulldozing uphill rather than down. While more time consuming and expensive, this method has several benefits.

"Most people want to clear a field of trees by pushing everything downhill. It's much easier," said Vinson. "But then their soil is downhill too, and the trees cleared are buried by the soil."

Hollifield makes the operator move everything uphill.

"To get those trees to the top, the dozer will do a better job knocking soil off the roots. He'd rather operate downhill, but you get everything in a draw, you can't do nothing with it," Hollifield said. "I'd rather

Left to right: Ken Deyton, Hollifield and Cliff Vinson look at young trees.

pay an extra $500 to save my soil and to get trees where we can use them.''

When asked if he had considered developing any of his land to profit from the tourist bonanza, he just laughed.

''Condominiums is a one-time crop,'' he said. ''You come back and find nothing but no trespassing signs. What do you do then?

''I like to stay busy,'' he said. ''I think it's good for a man to work. Exercise is good medicine. The more you're idle, the more you want to stay idle.''

A true farmer is seldom idle, and seldom wishes to be.

As Henry Beston once wrote, ''In all ages and in every nation, the farming population is the force which has bound human beings to reality and the earth . . . Without a farming population, a nation is never healthy of spirit.''

Frank Hollifield is one of those farmers who keep alive the values that made our country strong. His philosophy is a simple one we can all achieve: ''A man ought to enjoy life.''

FRESCOES

WEST JEFFERSON, N.C.—One of the great rewards for those who believe is to see faith in action.

In the isolated county of Ashe in the mountains of Western North Carolina, two small churches hold concrete examples of faith—frescoes glowing with love. To the mountain natives, the miraculous way in which these works arose has increased the number of parishioners from 13 to 300.

To the quarter of a million visitors who annually pass through these simple stuctures, the works of art mean much more than simply beautiful pictures.

Faith is at work.

When Father J. Faulton Hodge first came to the ministry of Ashe and Alleghany Counties in 1972, St. Mary's Episcopal Church was struggling along with only a handful of members. Holy Trinity Church was struggling to remain erect, but gradually losing the battle.

When he left in 1986, the churches were world famous and were supported by a strong and committed membership. The miracle happened naturally.

First, a chance meeting in 1973 at a party introduced Fr. Hodge to Ben Long, a native North Carolinian who had been living for several years in Florence, Italy, learning the technique of fresco painting. He was trying to find a church to work in.

"The host pointed out Long to Fr. Hodge and said that the artist would like to do a fresco in one of Hodge's churches. Fr. Hodge said that he couldn't even pay the light bill, much less art," says Virginia Meyers, manager of the gift shop at the Mission House at Holy Trinity Church.

"When the host said that Long would do it for free, Fr. Hodge said, 'Great, we'll take it. What's a fresco?' That's how it began," says Ms. Meyers.

A fresco is a form of painting in which the material of the wall— lime, sand, and mortar—are mixed with earth and mineral pigments to form a picture, which is part of the wall itself. It is an ancient art form practiced thousands of years ago by the Egyptians and best known in work by the Renaissance Italians.

Ben Long visited St. Mary's Church, trying to find a subject for his first fresco. While standing near the altar, he told Fr. Hodge that he felt a sense of great expectancy.

"This is St. Mary's Church—paint her expecting," responded the priest.

Using his own pregnant wife as the model for the figure and an unknown mountain girl as that for the face, Long created "Mary Great with Child." This fresco done in 1974 was the first of the series, and one of only three paintings in the world to depict Mary pregnant.

Today this work hangs in St. Mary's Church at Beaver's Creek with two more Long frescoes, "John the Baptist" and "The Mystery of Faith," which was completed in 1977.

In 1978, Fr. Hodge stood looking at the dilapidated structure of Holy Trinity Church, thinking that he might burn it and sell the property to raise money for the further restoration of his other church.

"I saw this large white car pull up, and an older man and his wife got out and came up to the church. The man asked what I was doing, and I told him I was the preacher, and I was thinking of tearing the church down. He asked why, and I said because I didn't have enough money to repair the main wall. He asked how much it would take, and I pulled a figure out of the air. I said $1500. The man took out his checkbook and wrote a check for most of that. And his wife gave me the rest," remembers Fr. Hodge.

Late that year restoration began, and by summer Ben Long and 23 artists from Europe and America had gathered to create his masterpiece, "The Lord's Supper."

Local people served as the models for the fresco, with Fr. Hodge included as the servant and Long using himself as a model for Doubting Thomas.

The local farmers and churches also fed the artists, who camped in the Mission House, in tents, and in a pickup truck. The creating of the work became as important as the finished product.

The resulting fresco glows with the faith that created it.

"It's a privilege to be able to worship in a place with those frescoes there. We are fortunate. During Holy Week we can observe services on Maundy Thursday right in front of the fresco 'The Lord's Supper.' On Good Friday at St. Mary's we worship in front of 'The Mystery of Faith,'" says Fr. Bill Pilcher, interim minister.

"My favorite part of 'The Lord's Supper' is the empty stool that stands in front of the table. The message is an invitation to become part of that scene with Jesus," says Fr. Pilcher.

Fr. Pilcher's mother, Camille Swan Pilcher of Johnson City, is typical of those who once see the churches of the frescoes; she returns again and again.

"She's an accomplished violinist; she and a friend came over in May to play at St. Mary's during services. She's been here several times," he says.

"The Last Supper" at Holy Trinity Church in Glendale Springs, NC.

Ben Scott of St. Petersburg, Florida, also recently returned to the churches.

"I'd say it's around the fourth time we've been here. We had some guests come to visit us and we brought them to see it. The paintings are inspiring, which is proven by the fact I keep coming back," says Scott.

His words are echoed by most who come to these simple country churches tucked back in the mountains.

Holy Trinity Church is located in Glendale Springs on highway 16 a short distance from the Blue Ridge Parkway. St. Mary's Church is just outside West Jefferson near US 221. For information write The Parish of the Holy Communion, Box 177, Glendale Springs, NC 28629 or call (919) 982-3076.

GEM MINING

LITTLE SWITZERLAND, N.C.—Be careful if you come to this quiet little town just off the parkway in Mitchell county. There's something catching, and it's dangerous because it never goes away.

It is Rockhound Fever—a fever that takes youngsters as quickly as seniors and everyone in between. Even the aloof disbelievers' eyes grow large and round at the first hint of something shiny, and they, too, are hooked.

"Look, Shelby, there's a huge amethyst, give it to Grandear," little seven-year-old Shelby Chandon's grandmother said with a squeal.

Grandear caught the fever with her first bucket of dirt-and-gemstone mix at the Emerald Village Gemstone Mine. She had actually bought the bucket for her granddaughter's entertainment but was soon gazing intently over the little girl's shoulder.

Cathy Schabilion, manager of Emerald Village, delights in seeing her customers find beautiful treasures as they sit at the sluice boxes and sift through buckets filled with dirt, rocks, gems and minerals.

"We guarantee that you'll find something in every bucket. Even though this area is rich in gems and minerals you just wouldn't find something in every bucket if you dug straight from the mine, so we enrich each bucket," Schabilion said.

The "buckets" range in price from three dollars to 100 dollars, depending upon the size, amount and type of gemstone you're looking for. Of course, the stones are in the rough still, but there are plenty of helpful employees around to help customers identify their finds.

"Any of the employees out here or in the shop can help with identification. We also have these displays which show what each thing looks like uncut and not polished," Schabilion said as she glanced over cases of blue, silver, and golden topaz, citrine, amethyst, tourmaline, quartz, emeralds, rubies, and other precious and semiprecious gems to be found in the wondrous buckets.

"We also have kyanite, amazonite, and moonstone. Those are really local things," Schabilion said.

Carolyn DePalma, of Lawrenceburg, Indiana, sat patiently sifting her stones. Although this was her first encounter with a gem mine, she was taking the work very seriously. DePalma scooped a shovelful of dirt into a screen-bottomed box, dipped the box in the water running through the sluice, and searched the remaining rocks for the colorful and shiny specimens sure to be there.

"This is my first time ever. I just enjoy gems. Today I've found citrine, garnets, amethysts. I don't know if I'll have any cut and mounted. I may just put them in a jar to look at. They are so pretty,'' Ms. DePalma said.

Gail Lyle and her children were vacationing in the mountains to get away from the piedmont heat in Hillsboro, North Carolina. She and the kids are hooked on gem hunting; you can see it in their eyes.

"This is about the fourth year we've looked for gems. I think it's something the children will always want to do," she said.

It is easy to believe that, once caught, rockhound fever lasts a lifetime. Just ask Claude McKinney who returns to the mine often.

"This place is like home to me. My father opened this mine just about 45 years ago, digging for feldspar. He could pretty well smell minerals. Of course they weren't looking for gems then," he said with a wry smile.

"They was looking for Dental Spar. That's right, back when they made false teeth out of 'spar. They dug it right out of this mine.''

McKinney looked around the pit, site of the present Emerald Village, and down toward the hole still in the side of the mountain.

"You get a love of the mining. I hope to give that to my grandsons," he said, standing beside Scottie and Matthew who each held a sack of minerals and gems found at the sluice.

"Claude has been a big help to us," Schabilion said. "He has shown us all around and helped us acquire relics for the mining museum we have across the road.''

In addition to the find-your-own area and the museum, Emerald Village has gift shops and on-site gem cutting and mounting.

The southern end of Mitchell County offers many gem mines, each with its own attraction. The Blue Ridge Gemstone Mine and Campground, well, it offers camping. Rio Doce is owned by Jerry Call, one of the area's many famous gem cutters.

Last fall Gem Mountain opened a new mine. They take their "miners" on field trips to a nearby mine.

"We furnish the transportation and all of the supplies you'll need like goggles, a hammer, and the sluice line to wash the rocks in," said Charles Buchanan, the owner.

"We were out mica mining last year when we found this gemstone mine. It's got aquamarine, golden beryl, garnets. What we do is blast some then haul it out and the visitors pick through it. They have to break the gems out of the rocks," he said.

The field trips last about two hours, with all but one-half hour spent at the mine, according to Buchanan.

"The mine is fifteen minutes from the shop here on (NC) 226," he said.

Shelby Chandon found a crystal

Emerald City and Ledford's are also located on NC 226 between Spruce Pine and the Blue Ridge Parkway. Emerald Village and neighboring Blue Ridge Gemstone Mine and Campground can be found by getting off the Parkway at mile post 334 and following the signs.

And while you're in the fever, don't miss the chance to stop in the free Museum of North Carolina Minerals, too. It is at the corner of the Parkway and NC 226. They have many interesting exhibits explaining why Mitchell County is one of the richest areas in gemstones and minerals in the continental United States.

Rockhounds at a sluice box

GRANDFATHER MOUNTAIN

GRANDFATHER MOUNTAIN, N. C.—Magic lives in the mountains, residing among the towering peaks thrust above the valley towns.

The Indians recognized this uplifting power and resorted to the high places to commune with the Great Spirit, and many men since have sought this solace.

Grandfather Mountain, at 5,964 feet the highest mountain in the Blue Ridge, has drawn seekers of natural wonder over the ages and continues to attract those escaping the hurly-burly of modern civilization.

Without the frantic rides and highly orchestrated entertainments of many mountain amusement areas, Grandfather Mountain hosts a steady flow of visitors entranced by the sights and sounds and feelings that no man has created.

"It's very simple," says Hugh Morton, principal owner and guardian of Grandfather. "We've got the prettiest mountain up here. Nothing in the way of manmade improvements can improve the beauty of the mountain.

"If we can preserve that beauty, we'll be going long after other people with their ferris wheels, neon lights, and cotton candy have gone out of business," he says.

As one of the oldest mountains in the world, Grandfather deserves its name, although its striking profile, which resembles that of an old man's face looking skyward, gave it that title. Strewn around the mountain are rocks and boulders formed over a billion years ago when the world was young.

Because of its southern location and high elevation, this ancient rock mass supports a wide variety of flora and fauna. Through the spring and summer a succession of flowers and birds and vibrant greenery together with the ever-changing weather makes each day on the mountain different.

The autumn brings the spectacular colors of the deciduous tree leaves, splashing the mountain's sides with multi-hued brilliance.

With the coming of winter, ice and snow create a more somber but no less striking beauty.

"We're trying to protect our mountain," Morton says. "There's a general feeling growing throughout the country and throughout the world that we've got to preserve the special shrines of nature."

While there is a road carved up the face of the mountain to the Nature Museum and on to "Mile High Swinging Bridge" and old visitor's center, most of the mountain remains free of "improvements," and

Bear Cubs

30 miles of hiking trails provide access to much of the unspoiled wilderness of Grandfather.

Morton sees himself as the guardian of the mountain's wild beauty and maintains a resolve to keep it from development that would destroy its character. It is his personal commitment to the mountain, he says.

One of the special features on the mountain is the environmental habitats, which provide visitors a chance to see some of the original denizens of the mountain in their natural environments.

"The environmental habitats kind of evolved," Morton remembers.

Invited to participate in a Black Bear replenishment program in 1968, Morton bought two bears from the Atlanta Zoo. The male and female were brought to the mountain where they were housed during the cold winter.

"In the spring we brought the male out. He stepped on a twig; it popped. We haven't seen him since," Morton recalls with a laugh. "We like to think that he's done his bit in repopulating the area."

The female bear, Mildred, when released showed a rather gregarious nature. She wandered through the populated areas near the mountain seeking the company of people.

"She was sticking her head through windows. Housewives screaming. Dogs barking," Morton says with laugh.

Declared a public nuisance in three counties, Mildred was brought home to Grandfather, where for a couple of years she was brought from her cage three times a day for the visitors.

"She's unquestionably the nicest bear that's ever been, so we decided we should have her continuously displayed. We had Bill Hoff, director of the North Carolina Zoo, and Hyatt Hammond the architect design a habitat," says Morton.

From that beginning, the program has expanded until now Grandfather has six environmental habitats.

The bear habitat is crowded with Mildred, her three grown cubs, Maxi, Mini, and Honey, and their friend, Hobo. A 10-foot wall rises from the floor of the enclosure to keep the bears from mingling with the visitors who look down from an elevated path. A cub habitat is separated from the main bear habitat.

A thousand-square-foot open air exhibit houses two bald eagles. The director of the Audubon Society's Eagle Propagation Program describes this as "the most beautiful open-air exhibit of flightless eagles to be found anywhere in the world." Two golden eagles live in a nearby habitat.

All these eagles have been shot or otherwise injured so that they can no longer fly. Hopes are that they will reproduce to send their eaglets soaring.

American Bald Eagles

Next door is the cougar habitat, and beside that an acre-and-a-half home for the whitetail deer. Joining the deer are ducks, groundhogs, and squirrels.

Various overlooks, the "Mile High Swinging Bridge," museum exhibitions and other mountain attractions make a visit to Grandfather Mountain a full one.

Everyone moves at his own pace without long lines, and there's no shoving on the swinging bridge.

Located on Highway 221 between the Blue Ridge Parkway and Linville, Grandfather Mountain opens its gates at 8 a.m.

SHEPHERD'S STAFF

SPRUCE PINE, N.C.—If you're out of luck in Mitchell County, you're in luck. There's a place to go when times are desperate. The Shepherd's Staff provides emergency assistance to anyone who is truly in need. Food, fuel, and financial aid, delivered with a warm smile and warmer sympathy, lift up the down-and-out and put them on their feet again.

"This is a place where anyone in need can get help, where people really do care," says Julia McPherson, director of Mitchell County Shepherd's Staff Inc. since March, 1984. She oversees this non-profit organization, guiding the efforts of the 40 to 50 volunteers and co-ordinating the incoming resources to maintain the outgoing aid.

In addition to her work at the combination office, used clothing store, thrift shop, and food bank, Mrs. McPherson makes speeches two or three times a month to encourage support of Shepherd's Staff. Her faith—always justified—keeps her from despair when funds run low. Their account has never hit rock bottom.

Local churches play an important role. The Ministerial Alliance founded Shepherd's Staff in 1983 to provide a central clearing house for emergency aid in the county. Today, under their Care and Share program, one of the alliance churches assumes responsibility for collecting food and contributions for one month a year on a rotating basis.

"Some churches are only interested in helping their own, but the others that work with us have the true Christian attitude that every man is their brother and deserves their help. These are our supporters and benefactors," the director says gratefully, pointing to the bulletin board list of 15 churches. The rest of the funding comes from United Way, the Community Fund, private donations, and receipts from sales of clothing and other items in the thrift shop.

To get aid, a person has only to deserve it. After an application is completed at Shepherd's Staff, the organization does the rest, whether finding food and shelter for the night for a penniless transient or filling a food box for a hungry local family.

Mrs. H. came in last winter. She had just been released from the hospital and found her money had been stolen and her electricity shut off for nonpayment. She was desperate. The letter of thanks she wrote tells the rest:

"I think you know what the $64.25 meant to me. It meant power for heating water, for cooking, for lights, for heating the house, etc. It really meant a lot to us. From our heart we thank you.

"But you did more. You went above and beyond the call of duty. As long as I live I will remember you and what you did."

The files at Shepherd's Staff are full of such stories. Like the one about the young man who had just got a job but wasn't allowed to work until he had a pair of steel-toed shoes. The $25 he received to buy the shoes put him on the payroll, enabling him to support his wife and two young children. He repaid the money out of his first paycheck.

Each month brings with it a parade of those at wit's end due to a variety of problems: someone is out of work, a husband has deserted his family, illness has cost a job, a Social Security check or food stamps have been stolen, hospital bills are eating up rent money—the list seems endless. And each month sees the distribution list grow.

The winter months are the most bitter. Jobs are scarce, but needs are many. Fuel is something that cannot be ignored when the temperature drops below freezing. Although fuel companies refuse to deliver less than $150 worth of heating oil and give no price break to charity, anyone in need is supplied from accumulated funds.

House fires occur more frequently during cold months. Burned-out families can pick any clothing or other household goods from the thrift shop free of charge, and the staff purchases any necessities—such as linens, blankets, and cookware—that might not be on the shelves.

During December, 22 families were chosen to receive Christmas baskets. "This place was like Santa's workshop," laughs Julia McPherson. "We cleaned and wrapped used toys and bought chicken, cakes, candy canes, oranges, nuts, and apples. It was wonderfully rewarding."

Of course, more help is needed. During the summer when calls for aid come less often, the staff prepares for the hard months ahead. Used goods are gathered for resale. And money can always be used. Any amount is appreciated. Three dollar bills once arrived in an envelope anonymously—an unexpected donation that Julia and her assistant Katy Putnam remember most fondly and gratefully.

The amount of aid provided by Shepherd's Staff cannot be judged merely in dollars and cents. In the first five months of this year, 195 families sought aid; $1,431 in financial assistance was dispersed, 110 food boxes containing 3,600 meals went to the hungry, five families were given lodging, 10 families received free clothing, and 15 meal vouchers were issued for transients to eat at the local hospital's cafeteria. Ask any of those helped if the little bit of money that it took to rescue him was important.

"The difficult thing for most people is swallowing their pride to ask for help; once they are here, we do everything we can to make them forget their problem and look forward to a better tomorrow," Mrs. McPherson said. "I really love people. You have to in this job. I try to pass on a warm smile with anything else we pass out."

So the next time you are near Spruce Pine, stop at the Shepherd's Staff. If you need help, you'll find it. If you don't, be thankful and pass on your good fortune. The shepherd's staff is extended to all.

LEVIE ODOM

BULADEAN, N.C.—Just before the century rolled over, Levie Greene Odom was born in the shadow of Roan Mountain. In the last 88 years she has seen Buladean and the surrounding area undergo some profound changes, but she has managed to preserve much of the important knowledge of simpler times.

Recently Levie has spent time telling her children, grandchildren, and great-grandchildren about a time with no cars, no electricity, no knowledge of canning. Dedee Odom, Levie's great-granddaughter, listened attentively as Levie told of an unimaginable time.

"When I was little there were no roads up in here, only branch beds with water running down them. My daddy, used to he always kept a team and wagon. He'd haul his apples and taters to Johnson City to peddle. It would take three days. And if he didn't sell his stuff out before Sunday, well he wasn't allowed to come back across the mountain. He had to lay over until Monday," Levie explained, alluding to the fact that absolutely no work was allowed on Sunday.

"They was strict on things back then."

Dedee could appreciate the difficulty of getting to the city and back from Levie's house on Blevins Branch. The old homeplace sits on the side of Roan Mountain. There's a two mile, dropping slope to Buladean, then about a six mile, steep climb to the top of the mountain pass and back down as much, or more to the foot of Iron Mountain on the Tennessee side and the fairly level 25 miles to the city.

The first time she went to Johnson City, the nearest large city to Buladean which lies on the North Carolina-Tennessee border, there were no cars, even in the city.

"They had lots of ponies and buggies, and lots of town folks would go of a Sunday afternoon and hire a pony and buggy and take a drive."

She can also remember a time when her mother had no knowledge of canning foods for winter. Then food was pickled and kept in jars or dried and kept in barrels.

"My daddy kept big stone jars for my mother to put things up in then. She'd pickle cucumbers, beans and such. 'Course, they dried beans and fruit, even blackberries," she said.

The family was nearly self-sufficient in those days. Her mother sewed clothes for the 11 children, some of whom died young, and her daddy made the shoes and ran a large farm.

In fact, in the early 1900s everyone had his work to do, even the children. When the weather turned warm under a new moon, Levie and a sister were given the task of plucking geese.

"My mother had 20 Indian Runner geese at one time. Sometimes a wing would get loose as we were a'plucking 'em and then flup, flup, flup—and them feathers'd go everywhere!" she remembered with the past in her eyes and light laughter in her voice. "And you had to get up every one, too. Needed 'em for beds and pillows."

Because she lost both of her parents by the time she was 18 (it was a hard time, when many died young), Levie found herself having to make a living of her own. First her grandmother took her in, then she kept house for a family in Erwin, Tennessee, earning $1 per week.

"I didn't get much, but then, things didn't cost you much. If you could buy your materials sometimes somebody'd make your clothes and not charge you for it. They was a lot of good hearted people then," she said.

Eventually Levie went to work at Veterans Administration Medical Center in Johnson City.

"I waitressed at the VA for $15 a month. I lived in a dormitory and was required to wear a uniform and cap all the time," she said. "Captain King, he ran the place and set the rules, he didn't allow us to go out with a boy, only twice a week. He was strict."

Levie didn't work at the VA for long. She returned to Buladean, where she fell in love with Sam Odom. She was then 21 years old.

"We rode horseback to Tennessee to get married. We had to go there because the man over there had the license," she said.

She and Sam had been married 53 years when he passed away in 1974.

Times weren't easy for the young couple, but with hard work and constant prayer, they got by as their eight children came along.

"We'd trade eggs and chickens for necessities in Buladean. One time I carried 101 eggs to the store. My arm was so sore!" she said.

More than once strong prayer and a good life paid off for Levie.

"There was one time, I added up the prices of what I needed and the prices of what I had to trade and I lacked 10 cents of having what I needed. We didn't go in debt at the store. Well, I'd already raided the hen's nest one time, but I thought, 'Well, maybe another hen's laid'. So, I went back up the path praying just as hard as I could, looking down at my feet, and if there didn't lay a new dime, just exactly what I wanted," she said.

"That dime meant more to me that day then $50 would today."

Today Levie lives comfortably in a house that sits not half a mile from where she was born. She has plenty of company since her daughter, Genevieve Odom, moved back in. Three of her other children live in Buladean, two in Johnson City, and two "live off now." Several times each year Levie and Genevieve hike to the woods to gather roots and plants for Levie's home remedies.

"I learned 'em from my mom. She taught me that peach leaves or bark make a good tonic for a bellyache, vomiting or when you're sick at your stomach. It's also a good cold remedy.

"I dry all kinds of mints for the winter, sassafras and spicewood for tea in the spring. Goldenseal is for ulcers, and slippery elm poultices help a bad bruise," she said.

Genevieve is trying to learn about the medicinal values of the forest plants so she can also pass them on one day.

"Momma's got a lot of valuable knowledge about this area—the people, plants, and history. You can't find most of what she knows in a book."

BLUEBERRIES

BAKERSVILLE, N.C.—There's something spiritually uplifting about standing on a mountainside early on a summer morning picking fat, juicy blueberries with no other thought than getting more in your bucket than in your belly.

If you are a blueberry lover, this is the time to venture out to the mountains to get the wonderful fruit. From Banner Elk to Buladean in North Carolina, or Unicoi in Tennessee, the blueberries are ready and waiting.

L. M. Faucette, of Colonial Hills Retirement Center in Johnson City, was picking berries one weekend at Blaine Hughes' family farm in Buladean. His buckets filled quickly as he talked about his yearly trips to pick blueberries in the mountains.

"I love to eat blueberries, but I also love to pick them. It becomes an outing. This is a nice place and it's a beautiful drive over here. A bit crooked for those not used to it, but beautiful," Faucette said.

Other pickers agreed with Faucette.

"This is a very nice patch. He's kept the rows mowed, the berries are easy to get to, and they're good berries. If I had my choice of pickin' berries, this would be it," said Kate Butt of Johnson City.

Another customer liked Hughes himself. "He's funny. He jokingly told us he'd weigh us in and weigh us out, so you better be careful how many you eat," said Margaret Hallaway also of Johnson City.

Hughes and his family are proud of their berries this year.

"These haven't been affected by the drought. I irrigated so that we'd have a good crop, and it paid off. I piped pure spring water from under The Roan, piped it down 300 feet to irrigate these plants," Hughes said.

Most farmers have had to irrigate this year in order to keep their crops alive, according to Ken Deyton with the U.S. Soil Conservation Service. Arnold and Betty Odom who live just over the ridge from the Hughes' farm also used spring water to irrigate their berries.

"They are so big and so juicy. I guess they wouldn't've been if we hadn't watered 'em. But we ended up with a good crop," Mrs. Odom said.

The Banner Elk growers were not spared by the drought either. The owners of the Blue Ridge Blueberry Farm also had to irrigate in order to have a healthy crop.

"We have plenty of berries and they're big. We irrigated and then we've had some good rains over the last week. People like to come here for a day of good fun, picking, enjoying the mountains, meeting other pickers who swap recipes,'' said Betty Kelsey who, along with husband Jack, owns and operates the farm.

Hughes explained why the mountain berries are so sweet.

"I've been told, 'to find where to grow blueberries look for the indication plants.' Those would be laurel, wild azalea, rhododendron. You know, that's where you find the natural blueberry plants, the huckleberries as some calls 'em,'' he said as he pointed to the woods near the blueberry patch, indicating that those plants grew nearby.

While Hughes enjoys his work, he doesn't recommend it to everyone, "I think its worth it, if it's something you like to do. I like to plant things and watch them give fruit, but there's a lot involved in it. It takes five years before you get a good crop. All that time there's the mowing, pruning, you know just like if they were producing.''

For those who would rather let others do the farming, there are several places you can go to either pick your own blueberries or buy them just-picked. In Tennessee the Boones, Mamie and Jim, have a farm on Highway 107 in Unicoi County. Mamie said that they would be ready for buyers to come out in the next week.

"We've just bought a mechanical picker so I think we'll just have berries and berries to sell. At least I hope it'll work the way it's supposed to. So we won't have any pick your own, but we'll have plenty to sell,'' she said.

In Banner Elk the Kelseys will pick for you or let you pick for yourself. Mrs. Kelsey said that pickers should bring their own containers to carry them home in, preferably a shallow, flat carton so that the air can circulate and so that they don't crush under their own weight. The Kelseys are 1 and 7/10ths miles east of the traffic light in Banner Elk, on Lee Gualtney Road.

"We even have our own blueberry honey—the nectar was gathered from the blueberry blossoms,'' she said.

Along NC 226 in Buladean there are signs directing traffic to many small blueberry farms. The Hughes farm is on Odom's Chapel Road, off Hughes Gap Road which turns east off of NC 226.

After Hughes Gap Road, the next road to the east is Blevins Branch, where the Odoms have their berry patch high on the side of Roan Mountain. While you have to pay for the berries, the view is free.

For the names of more upper Mitchell County blueberry growers, contact the Agriculture Extension Office at (704) 688-2051.

BETTY KELSEY'S BLUEBERRY-OAT MUFFINS

3 cups Bisquik
½ cup packed brown sugar
¾ cup quick cook oatmeal
1 tsp. ground cinnamon
2 eggs well beaten
1½ cups milk
¼ cup melted butter
2 cups fresh blueberries

Combine Bisquik, brown sugar, oatmeal and cinnamon. In separate bowl mix eggs, milk and butter. Add dry ingredients all at once and stir until blended. Fold in berries. Spoon into greased muffin tin, ¾ full. Bake in 400 degree oven for 15-20 min. or until golden brown. Remove from pans immediately and serve warm.

MARGARET HUGHES' EASY BLUEBERRY PIE

2 cups frozen blueberries, thawed and drained
1½ cups sugar
juice of ½ orange
2 tbsp. cornstarch
1 baked 8 inch pie shell
1½ cups fresh blueberries

Cook thawed berries in 1½ cups water for 5 min. Add sugar and orange juice. Cook for 5 min. longer. Combine cornstarch and ¼ cup cold water, mix well. Add cornstarch mixture to blueberry mixture, stirring until thickened. Remove from heat; cool slightly. Pour into pie shell. Cover with fresh blueberries. Serve cold with whipped cream or ice cream.

MAMIE BOONE'S DEEP DISH BLUEBERRY PIE

6 cups fresh blueberries
1 cup sugar
1 cup corn starch
3 tbsp. lemon juice
3 or 4 tbsp. butter

Prepare pastry for two-crust pie. Line greased baking dish (ceramic) with pastry. Combine washed berries with other ingredients except butter and put in pastry. Dot with butter. Top with remaining rolled pastry. Seal edges, making small slits in top for ventilation. Place in 400 degree oven for 15 min. Lower to 350 degrees and continue to bake for 45 min. Serve hot or cold with whipped cream.

HANNAH MILLER'S BLUEBERRY DUMPLINGS

1 quart blueberries
1 teacup sugar
½ cup water
any biscuit dough

Place berries, sugar and water in a deep pot. Bring to a boil. Drop balls of uncooked biscuit dough into boiling mixture. Cover and allow to boil gently until biscuits (dumplings) are steamed. Serve with whipped cream or vanilla ice cream.

ZEDA PARKER'S BLUEBERRY YUM-YUM

3 cups graham cracker crumbs
1 8-oz. pkg. cream cheese
1½ sticks softened butter or margarine
blueberry filling*
2 large tubs Cool Whip
    * 3 tbsp cornstarch
      ½ cup water
      ½ cup sugar
      2 cups blueberries

Make filling by boiling water, sugar and cornstarch. Take off heat and add berries.

Mix crumbs and softened margarine together. In separate bowl mix cream cheese and Cool Whip. Press ½ crumb mixture in bottom of ungreased Pyrex dish. Spread ½ Cool Whip over crumbs. Next spread all of blueberry filling over Cool Whip. Spread remaining Cool Whip and sprinkle remaining crumbs over top. Refrigerate for 3 hours or more.

HOLT GRIFFITH: WEATHER WATCHER

TIPTON HILL, N.C.—Everyone complains about the weather, but no one does anything about it. No one but Holt Griffith, at any rate.

This retired minister, dairyman, carpenter, and woodwork-and-carpentry teacher keeps a daily journal in which he notes meteorological information, as well as important local events, deaths, etc.

Beginning about 20 years ago, Griffith, who at 72 lives on the same piece of land he crawled over as a baby, has kept records of the area's precipitation and other data.

No one knows better than he how severe is this year's drought.

"There's nothing to compare with it," he said, opening the blue diary in which he has noted the last two years of his data. "Right now we have 18.45 inches for the year. Last year at this time we'd had 29.15 inches, and that was a dry year.

"In fact, it's gradually been falling for years. In the '60s one year it went to 72 inches, which was about normal for when I was a boy," he recalled. "It stayed in the 60-inch range for a number of years. In the last 10 to 12 years it's fell into the 50s, about 55 inches as an average.

"This year's the lowest I've ever known it. Nothing to compare with it."

With his diversity of careers, Griffith has proven his own adage, "the weather governs you in just about everything you go at." Whether raising a house as a carpenter, pasturing his cows as a dairyman, planning a "burying" as a preacher or a class as a carpentry teacher, he's had to work with the weather to adjust to its changing conditions.

This year Griffith's garden is as successful as any and more so than most, because over the past few years of gradually diminishing precipitation he has rigged an irrigation system to keep his crops well watered.

As he raked a mess of fist-sized potatoes from one hill, he explained how he "does something about the weather."

"I've watched my water carefully; streams that I never knew to go dry have this year," he said. "So today I water with the sprinkler for 20 minutes, then let the reservoir fill for 40 to fill back up. In the past I could water for 35 minutes with only 25 to fill the 200 gallon reservoir."

Griffith is already preparing for this coming winter, counting the fogs in August (he's up to nine) to determine the number of snows he'll see during the cold months.

"Last year in August we had 18 days with fog. One day with two—foggy in the morning, then in the afternoon fog came right through the gap and filled the valley," he said, leafing through his book. "We had 19 snows last winter."

"In 1984 we had 24 fogs with 26 snows. I've found it down through the years to show up a variation of two between the numbers," he said, brandishing a handful of small journals in irrefutable support.

While many men retire to the sofa and television set, Griffith has used his time to watch and learn more about the weather.

"Time and time again I'll sit here and watch rain fall at the head of the valley. The clouds fill over the ridge; it's the main dividing ridge between Rock Creek and Tennessee. But it will be just as dry down here," he said. "It's interesting to watch the weather. And a man needs to know it."

With his rain gauge, his high-low thermometer, and his observant eye, Holt Griffith maintains his ever-swelling collection of record books.

"You never think how valuable these records can be, but hardly a week goes by but somebody calls me to ask about a day, and I get out that little book to check," he says proudly.

BLACK MOUNTAIN CAMPGROUND

MICAVILLE, N. C.—"There's something about the feel of this place. It has an attitude."

Dr. Davey Haughton's description of the Black Mountain Campground is vague and confusing until you've spent several hours there.

Haughton, from West Palm Beach, Florida, was camping last week at the Black Mountain Campground for the second time. He spoke of the place with the same enthusiasm that most visitors show.

"It is one of the premier camping spots in the country. It's the whole combination you get here, the river, the good people, the lay of the campground, and just the atmosphere," he said.

Located off Highway 80 South, the campground, run by the U.S. Forest Service, offers cool shade, cool water, some facilities, and privacy.

Each of the 48 camping spaces has a tent pad, a picnic table, a barbecue grill, and a below-ground garbage can. Most are surrounded by large, old trees which provide shade and privacy at each site. Drinking water is available at several locations in the park, though not at every site.

The gentle breeze blowing constantly off the South Toe River which runs along the eastern border of the campground combines with the plentiful shade to keep the campground cool, even on the hottest days. While the campground offers no officially designated swimming areas or lifeguards, visitors find plenty of places along the river with holes deep enough to swim in.

"It's really a fishing stream. We don't have any swimming areas, but the kids and adults alike always find water deep enough for swimming," said Lee Thompson with the Forest Service.

Fourteen-year-old Jason Smith from Kannapolis, North Carolina, has been coming to the campground with his parents and grandparents since he was a little baby. He especially enjoys the park because there are plenty of things for a teenager to do.

"There's swimming at the river, hiking on the trails, and there's a bike trail. I get to see a lot of the same people every year, too," Jason said.

While Jason enjoys the activities the campground has to offer, he also likes the natural settings of each campsite.

"It's like camping by yourself. You don't have electricity, paved roads, you don't see the campers at the next site," he said.

"Yeah, it's REAL camping," chimed in Jason's friend Brian Rhodes, 12, of Forest City, North Carolina. For the last two years the boys' families have met, by accident, at the campground.

The Drew family from Ridgeland, South Carolina, returned to the campground this summer because they had had such a good time last year. Even 17-year-old Lee likes this campground.

"There's definitely enough to do, even for us older kids. But I'd have to say that Jamie likes it best. He runs, jumps, swims and splashes the whole time he's here," Lee said.

True to his brother's description, eight-year-old Jamie ran past, shouting an invitation for everyone to join him at the waterfall.

"The waterfall comes in handy," Thompson said. "There are three bathrooms around the campground, but they aren't equipped with showers. So, folks like to go down to the waterfall to rinse off after a hot day."

At the back of the campground is an area called Briar Bottom which offers group camping. Each site consists of enough room and facilities for 50 campers. Advance reservations for Briar Bottom must be made at the Forest Service office in Burnsville (704) 682-6146.

"Briar Bottom used to be this campground's best kept secret. Now quite a few church groups come, many from Charlotte," said Jason Smith's grandmother, Janet Fowler.

Grandpa Joel (Fowler) and his wife first came here to camp in 1939 or '40. They know the campground and surrounding mountains well.

"It hasn't changed here at all. It's still quiet and cool. There used to be a trout down there" (hands held a foot-and-a-half apart) "this big. He had a hook in his mouth. The water was so clear you could see him swimming around. The water's still clear, but I haven't seen that fish lately," Fowler said.

The campground hosts, Gertie and Lewis McIntyre, are friendly and helpful. Lewis spends much of his time on the front porch of the Forest Service trailer at the front of the campground. He greets the campers with a wave and is available to assist in any way, but he doesn't push himself on the guests.

Gertie spends a little more time walking around the park, checking on the campers, making sure that everyone has remembered to register, knows where to get water, and how to get to the river.

The McIntyres have been hosts at this campground for four summers. Both say they absolutely love it.

"I love it here first of all because it is the place I was born and raised— just up the road. Most of the time it is nice and cool here and there's never any trouble. We come here and have a good time," Gertie said.

The McIntyres arrive at the campground on Thursday of each week and stay until Monday afternoon, but the campground is open all week long. Lewis warned that visitors ought to arrive by midday on Thursday to insure a good campsite.

"It fills up pretty quickly here on the weekends," he said.

Camping is on the honor system, $6 per site, per night; senior citizens get a half price discount. Check-out time is two o'clock p.m., with a maximum stay of 14 days.

To find the campground take NC Highway 80 S to the Mt. Mitchell Golf Course. Forest Service signs direct campers to the campground entrance where a bulletin board gives further directions.

GINSENG THIEF

BULADEAN, N.C.—One late August Sunday morning a stranger in a cream colored pickup drove up the dirt road along Greasy Creek. By that evening most of the ginseng plants in the valley were gone, rudely ripped from the soil. Large and small, mature and immature, gone.

What makes a man ruin the very thing he seeks? The ginseng plant has flourished in these mountains long before man roamed them, yet because many shortsighted, greedy collectors have ravished the slopes of the young plants as well as the older, seed-bearing ones, many coves are completely barren of this long-cherished perennial.

Late that afternoon I came upon several plots in the woods that had been roughly hoed up, the tops thrown to the side. Small one- and two-leaf seedlings lay beside the foot-tall, four-pronged mature plants with their clusters of green seeds.

These seeds, though not ripe, might have a chance to germinate to renew the crop; however, another year with such an assault and the plants will be gone from this valley. And no one will ever again gather ginseng from the forest above Greasy Creek.

There are laws to protect the plant, yet few bother to learn them and even fewer follow them. The season for gathering the plant doesn't open until August 30. Waiting until this date gives the seeds a chance to develop.

No one should harvest the plant until the berries are ripe, bright red, bursting. Then the ginseng has a chance to replenish itself if the forager will leave the seed top in the hole from which he has dug the root, or if he will plant the berries an inch or so under the surface.

Only those plants with seeds should be taken. First, these are the plants with roots mature enough to justify their collection; but, more importantly, all ginseng should be given an opportunity to reproduce. Only then will there be ensured a crop for the next year, and the next.

What kind of selfishness could motivate a man to ruin the very harvest he seeks, not only for himself in the future, but for all coming generations? Once the plants are gone from the wild, they are gone. No amount of searching will yield a harvest if the woods are barren.

If you go into the mountains to search for ginseng, think before you dig. Don't destroy a part of mountain heritage that has yielded a joyful harvest for generations.

Leave the seeds. Leave the small plants. There will be something to come back for next year.

Ginseng plant with berries

MOUNT PISGAH

MOUNT PISGAH, N.C.—Few places on the Blue Ridge Parkway bring together as much as Mount Pisgah. Hiking trails, campgrounds, picnic areas, a first class restaurant, an inn, a 360 degree vista, natural beauty, and even a television transmission tower provide something of interest for everyone.

Mount Pisgah at 5,749 feet is not the highest but is one of the most recognizable of the mountain peaks in Western North Carolina, for it thrusts above its surroundings so clearly. From the Asheville area it is the most prominent mountain on the skyline.

In her 1876 novel, **The Land of the Sky**, Christian Reid describes its appearance in glowing terms as her mountain visitors approach Asheville:

"We find ourselves facing a great pomp of sunset. In the midst of it rises, like a dream of the celestial country, a glorified azure peak of exquisite symmetry, and Eric says, 'Pisgah'!"

Of course, the Biblical associations of the name **Pisgah** reveal the religious nature of the early mountain folks. Led by the Lord, Moses first viewed the promised land from the top of Mt. Pisgah near the Dead Sea.

The "land of milk and honey" that underlies the Appalachian Mt. Pisgah on all sides obviously recalled to some early explorer of the mountain the land of plenty that awaited the Israelites.

Two different men are cited as the sources of the name: a chaplain, James Hall, who accompanied an early military expedition in 1776 and Rev. George Newton, a Presbyterian minister who founded Newton Academy in Asheville.

By 1800 the name Pisgah was firmly established for the peak.

Throughout the 19th century it figured in the history of the area. Given to the controversial politician, general, and mountain explorer Thomas Clingman so that he could qualify as a landowner to run for state senator, Mt. Pisgah was later purchased from him by George Vanderbilt as the centerpiece for the forest of his estate, Biltmore.

Eventually the mountain passed to the U. S. Forest Service to serve as the nucleus for the Pisgah National Forest in 1914.

Today the Blue Ridge Parkway runs along the Pisgah Ridge, and the peak is easily accessible to anyone with the energy to hike 1.5 miles, mountain miles.

"It's great exercise. You really get your heart pumping and sustain it for the entire walk up," says Hunter Jerome about the hike.

Tower atop Mt. Pisgah

The trail to the top begins with an easy level section, but towards the end the trail becomes a trial as it climbs steeply through the laurel and rhododendron bushes. An observation deck with an extensive open vista awaits the successful hiker.

On a clear day, Tennessee, North and South Carolina, Georgia, and range after range of mountains and peaceful surrounding valleys draw the eye. This is the view that gave the mountain its name and has attracted lovers of natural beauty for hundreds of years.

On a cloudy day, the massive television transmission tower of WLOS in Asheville becomes the main attraction to catch the visitors' attention. It stands directly beside the observation deck.

While not a natural beauty, its ponderous size is difficult to ignore. Although stern signs warn against climbing the tower, few hikers can resist at least walking around the structure and marvelling.

Charles Brinkley, his wife Sheila and daughter Heather recently made the hike to the top with their dogs, Stormy, Sheba and Ginger. They were on a day trip from Winston Salem, North Carolina.

"We enjoy the hike up, and the dogs do, too. We try to get up every year," said Charles Brinkley, as he and his troop rested on the rocks under the tower.

The Kerr clan from Fort Lauderdale, Florida, also enjoyed the hike up. Father William and sons Billy and Bobby were staying in the Pisgah Inn which could barely be seen through the mist when the clouds parted for a moment.

"It's beautiful up here, even when the clouds are thick," said Mr. Kerr, as the boys sampled the provisions that they had brought along to sustain them on the hike.

For those without the foresight to bring their own food, the Pisgah Inn can satisfy the appetite created by the hike. The Inn offers both a coffee shop and a quality restaurant serving fresh trout, prime rib, country ham, chicken cordon bleu and many other tasty dishes.

The Inn also has rooms with a view—the kind of view that few hotels in the world can offer. At 5,000 feet, the Inn provides a spectacular sunrise to sunset look at the world below.

Campgrounds with 120 campsites, picnic areas, a gas station, gift shop, and more hiking trails (one with a botanical tour) make the Mt. Pisgah stop one with something for everyone.

"This time of year the visitors are fairly evenly spaced," said Ranger Cliff Kevill as he worked to unlock the door of a hiker whose girl friend had locked his keys in the car.

"The busiest days of the year are the weekends in October when the fall color is at its peak. Now the campground usually isn't filled up,

Bobby Kerr

but then it may be. It's first come, first serve,'' he said, then smiled triumphantly as the door came open.

Mt. Pisgah is located south of Asheville on the Blue Ridge Parkway at milepost 408.

For information or reservations write Pisgah Inn, P.O. Box 749, Waynesville, NC 28786 or call (704) 235-8228.

WAGON TRAIN

BULADEAN, N.C.—The clip-clop of steel shod hooves and the screech of iron tires on asphalt gave way to a muffled tread and the crunch of gravel as the wagon train crossed the line from Tennessee into North Carolina at Hughes Gap one Saturday afternoon.

The men and the beasts breathed a sigh of relief. The long steep climb from Burbank was over; it was all downhill from here.

Starting early that morning from the Doe River Gorge between Hampton and Roan Mountain, the horses, mules, wagons, and men, women and children were tired. So was the dog; Trouble had been running beside the wagons for the full trip.

There were still several miles to go to camp. But the leader was not worried. Johnny Reed had picked his company with care.

"I sort 'em out. See, you gotta be a little bit tough to go for two or three days on a wagon train. It's not much fun to have a bunch of people whining, or stock sick and lame.

"I make sure everybody works their stock. Our stock don't have no sores on 'em. You only see prime stock here," Reed said, pointing to his own four mules in flashing harness.

The wagon train moved steadily through Buladean. Local farmers and horse fanciers stopped work to admire the quality horses and mules and their proud owners.

Despite their evident enjoyment of the ride, everyone was glad to reach the campground at Jack Hopson's field across from his store.

"We came about twenty miles today. I rode horseback the whole way. It's a ball; it always is when we get out and ride," said Rocky Whittington, a pretty girl under a black Stetson.

Camp quickly fell into place. Everyone pitched in. Children helped their parents strip the harness from the the teams, then tied out the stock and stacked the gear. Hay was provided for the hardworking beasts, and everyone began to relax and talk.

"We've been going on wagon trains for over 15 years. We started with a one horse wagon," said Stanley Largent from Whitehead Hill.

"I was born and raised with it, horses and mules. My father, grandfather, great-grandfather—as far back as anyone can remember—my family always farmed and raised horses, logged with horses, too," said Johnny Reed.

As Randy McKinney's young Belgians relaxed, the harness lines sweated into their hides gradually began to fade. The Roan Mountain farmer patted his dog Trouble.

Johnny Reed's 4-mule team leads the wagon train.

Some members of the wagon train rode horseback for the entire 20-mile trip.

Everyone was glad to reach camp at the end of the day.

The Manns' Belgians share supper.

"He ran all the way. I wouldn't take nothing for this dog," he said.

The youngsters kept an eye on the stock. One boy, David Stevens, dashed about on a different horse or mule every few minutes. What is fantasy for most boys is his reality.

Even newcomers to the world of two-horsepower transportation seemed to settle right in.

"I converted my husband Shane from motorcycles to horses. This team was my father's, and when he passed on we got them to keep them in the family," said Nina Sue Mann as she cooked their supper over a flaming barbecue grill.

Shane smiled and took a sip of a mountain beverage, then offered it to his buddy.

"Yeah, it's a great life on the wagon train," he said, his smile broadening.

Rocky's banjo provided the harmony for the scattered conversations. Tired children nestled close to their parents. Barbecue fires hissed in the dark.

"It's really a family thing. Everyone has something to do and enjoys doing it. A lot of people would be better off if they were on wagon trains," said Johnny Reed.

"It's a lot of fun. A lot of hard work, but a lot of fun. We ride about every weekend. On my first date with Johnny we went riding. We've been riding ever since," said Maggie Reed.

"I've done the wagon train since I was a baby. I love being with the horses and the people," said their daughter Patty.

As night settled upon the camp and laterns lit the white canopies of the covered wagons, Jack Hobson's field seemed a good place to be, and the life of a wagoneer a good one to live.

Sunday morning the rising mist found the people of the wagon train harnessing the horses and mules and stowing their gear. The trail led up through Iron Mountain Gap, and it was time to get going.

Harnesses stacked carefully before supper.

GARRETT ARWOOD

PIGEON ROOST, N.C.—If you drive up the narrow road that climbs through this isolated part of Mitchell County and listen carefully, you might hear the sweet sounds of a mountain fiddle drifting on the breeze.

It'll be Garrett Arwood, fiddling around.

To know the story of Southern Appalachia, pay a visit to Arwood and ask to hear his life story. It's a primer of mountain life in the twentieth century.

Born on the same plot of land that he now occupies, Arwood had to leave his home for 29 years to take his family to seek a livelihood in the industrial midwest. But his mountain roots never tore loose.

Today at the age of 83, Garrett Arwood spends his time in the home he built for himself and his wife just behind the old homestead. There he makes fiddles in the true mountain way—with ingenuity, hard work and pride.

He learned to make fiddles the same way he learned to play them, figuring it out for himself.

"My brother-in-law Marsh Miller, he lives on Dry Creek over in Unicoi, brought me a fiddle that had come apart from the damp. It was an old fiddle, and back then the glue wasn't as good as it is now—didn't hold like it does now," Arwood says.

"I fixed that fiddle, making the molds myself, then got to repairing all kinds of fiddles. I'd look them over and see the different designs and figure it out from there," he says. "Then I decided if I could fix one, I could make one."

Today, 55 fiddles later, Arwood has the reputation of a master craftsman with the fiddle. The **Foxfire Book IV** features Arwood and his fiddle-making skills, and fiddle players from all around are happy to get an Arwood instrument.

Not only are the fiddles themselves handmade, but the tools and molds Arwood uses are also home-invented and hand-constructed. A visit to his workroom is a lesson in humility for anyone who has ever found any job too intricate to figure out or too difficult to complete.

His lathe for turning the tuning keys is constructed from a ¼ inch drill, a large screw, and clamps. His molds for forming the precisely curved sideboards of his fiddles are contrived from wood, screws and expertise. His gouging tools are made from mill files. His smallest blade started out as a jigsaw blade.

"This comes in real handy," he says, holding the small implement. "I made it out of a jigsaw blade. Cut the teeth out of it and stuck it in the handle."

Arwood examines a hand-carved fiddle handle.

When asked how he ever came up with the ideas and the skill to turn those ideas into workable tools, Arwood just smiles.

"These things you can do if you make up your mind and do it," he explains.

"I wasn't ever no little wizard. Most of the work I did was common labor—farm work, sawmill hand, brickwork, delivering coal. I like to work," he says.

His philosophy and skills are the products of his birth and nurturing. His ability to make do and do well comes from his heritage and his life.

"All of us mountain people come from countries where they're intelligent people. We all had to live on our own and had to do the things needed to live. A person who grew up and had to work, knows how," Arwood says.

"My daddy and mommy had 12 children and raised all but one, David, who died at 3. People had to work to raise that many children.

"The living came mainly from the little farms. They'd take 'em out to work when just a bitty thing—five or six-year-old. Working then was as important as schooling. We went to school just below here."

"I didn't get much education. Back then teachers didn't force you to learn everything. I got some things up to the 4th grade, some things up to the 8th grade. Mostly I've had to teach myself," he says.

Arwood and his family got by doing farm work and taking advantage of any opportunity to make a little money. Working at the local sawmill, collecting acid wood, peeling bark from chestnuts for tanning, and selling pulpwood provided their cash until the Great Depression.

"I went North during that terrible depression, and I was lucky and got work. There was no work here and hardly any work there, but we'd do anything they had that needed doing. Some men up there would only do certain things," Arwood says.

For 29 years Arwood labored at one job or another, doing what there was to do, and doing it well. But he always felt the pull of his homeland.

"Yes, we missed the mountains. You think about these hills and how you lived. When the last place I worked in Illinois closed down, we decided to come home," he says.

Back in Pigeon Roost, Arwood bought the old family homestead from his brother, then built the house he and his wife Nora live in. They restored the farm, making it productive once again.

In the early 1970s, Arwood began to make fiddles. He's never stopped. And playing them is his favorite pastime.

"Factories can turn 'em out faster. Sometimes they sound good; sometimes they don't," Arwood says. "They'll do some things all right, but then do other parts poorly."

Garrett Arwood takes the time to do his fiddle-making right. The soundboards are made from spruce, the rest of the body from curly maple. The keys and fingerboard are made of walnut, and the head is handcarved. To string his bows he uses horsehair taken from the tails of mountain horses.

His fiddles are beautiful to look at and a joy to hear.

When Garrett Arwood plays a tune on his own instrument, the essence of the mountains rises from the vibrating strings like mist from the valley.

No trick of training can bring to "Little Maggie" or "Little Log Cabin in the Lane" or "Twilight Is Stealing" the depth and sweetness that Garrett Arwood creates with his handmade fiddle and his lifetime of joys and sorrows.

If you need a good fiddle or simply a taste of mountain life, call on Garrett Arwood. It's worth a trip to Pigeon Roost just to hear him play.

DECORATION

BULADEAN, N.C.—Throughout the mountains of Western North Carolina and East Tennessee, small family graveyards crown knolls or sit comfortably near country churches or among old farmsteads. Once a year many of these cemeteries draw families together for reunion and celebration.

Known as "Decorations," these gatherings both bring extended families together and keep the burial places in good condition.

Each year the Hughes family gathers in Buladean for their annual Decoration.

The grass closely clipped, the gray stones carefully cleaned, and the bright flowers skillfully arranged, the cemetery becomes the focus for the almost 200 members of the family.

"The main thing is the 11 o'clock service and preaching at the cemetery," said Ethel Hughes Ollis. "The graves are decorated before; some come on Saturday to decorate. We have the service to remember our family dead."

Under the gloom of heavy clouds, the gray stones dominated the cemetery as the family gathered in 1986, but when the service began, the sun broke through intermittently to strike life from the bright dahlias, hydrangeas, and chrysanthemums, those same stones becoming the background for the flaming flowers.

In the same way, the usually ominous presence of death in the graveyard surrendered to the vital flow of love and life of the Hughes family.

For over 50 years this family has met in the same cemetery on the fourth Sunday in August to honor its dead. Dave Hughes, who now occupies a plot next to his wife Hannah, began the custom, joining the Decoration to an annual family dinner that began almost a century ago.

The service began with music, the Montgomery family singing traditional gospel songs.

"We were neighbors of Zeda (one of Dave Hughes' daughters), and we really got to know her well. She was shut in for a long time in her sickness, and we went in and sang to her," John Montgomery said.

For Zeda's five grandchildren and 10 great-grandchildren, the Montgomerys sang her favorite song, "Mother's Dying Message."

Roy Whitson from the nearby Roan's Chapel Freewill Baptist Church preached some words of comfort: "When the grave finds us, it's the beginning of a brand new life for them that love the Lord. We can learn lessons from these dead. We all know them. All these" (his gaze swept the glowing cemetery) "examples are clear."

To this mountain family, the dead are not "dead and gone," but "dead and gone to a better place." They live on in the spirit and are felt as living presences.

The tears spilled are not bitter, but joyous ones, for the mood is celebratory, not mournful. Memories recalled are living ones.

Dave Hughes and his wife Hannah provided the land for this cemetery in 1924 to bury their son Gibbs, who was its first occupant. Since that time many members of the family have joined him.

The bright flowers are meant to cheer not only the survivors but also their dead.

"My daddy (Dave) was a lover of flowers. As long as I can remember he raised 'em," recalled Lee Hughes, who at 78 is the present patriarch of the clan. "For the graves he especially raised dahlias."

Mrs. Ollis agreed, "There's a tradition of raising dahlias for the Decoration. But this year they are so scarce because of the drought."

However, the scarcity did not show, for an abundance of blossoms outlined each plot and sent messages to Hugheses gone before.

Younger generations of the Hughes family are proud of their family traditions and respect their forebears deeply. The importance of the Decoration is not lost on them.

"There's graveyards all over the mountains here. Some are growed up and forgotten. We don't want that to happen to ours," said Jones Hughes, son of Lee and grandson of Dave.

"There's an old grave up in the woods. My Aunt Vista is buried there. She was born in 1896 and died at the age of seven, 48 years before I was born. This October we're going to exhume her body and bury her with a tombstone in this cemetery," he said.

"All her nephews cares enough to want her moved. All my aunts and uncles that I can remember, we nephews have been pallbearers. We care about the family," Jones said.

Surrounding the graves of Dave and Hannah and the rest of their dead were four of their surviving children, 18 of their grandchildren, 35 of their great-grandchildren, and 17 of their great-great-grandchildren.

The oldest to attend was 87-year-old Levie Odom; the youngest, newborn Isaac Ollis.

Following the service, the family walked through an apple orchard to Garland Hughes' house, which sits on the site of the old family homestead, to enjoy a bountiful feast.

"My daddy loved to cook for folks. He liked nothing better than to have a houseful waiting for his biscuits," remembered Lee. "Before even the Decoration began back in the '30s, the family'd gather for a big feast at the end of August."

"Grandpa sometimes would catch a pig in the mountains and put it up to fatten for awhile, then prepare it on an open fire all day and all night just for the occasion," said Jones Hughes. "Every kind of food was fixed and in quantity."

The tradition continues. Two heaped tables extended out both ends of the carport, and everyone from great-grandmothers to toddlers enjoyed the bounty and the chance to talk with relatives gathered from throughout the country.

While many lingered over the meal and the teIllowship, others paid a last visit to the cemetery. The quick and the dead joined in celebration of family.

Many old customs survive among the mountain families of the Southern Appalachians, but the one that best epitomizes their deep faith and the strong ties that bind is the Decoration.

For the the Hughes family the cemetery is not a dread place, but the well-chosen resting spot for those whose work is done.

Family patriarch Lee Hughes stands between his parents' graves.

Wes Hoilman

WES HOILMAN'S CHEVROLET SAWMILL

MICAVILLE, N.C.—As the chill of fall begins to fill the hollows and hover around the peaks of the Southern Appalachians, mountain folks' thoughts turn to their woodpiles. For many, a warm fire is more than an amenity, it's a downright necessity.

For Wes Hoilman, keeping a good stock of wood is a foregone conclusion. There is no choice.

"All my heat is wood, and I cook with wood," he says, looking as if there is no other way.

With typical mountain ingenuity, Hoilman has rigged himself a device to make keeping that woodpile stocked an easier chore. Wasted motion and effort are left to youth; he is happy to get the most done with the least toil.

Sitting in front of his house is a hybrid contraption that looks like a car from the front but a sawmill from the back. It is a little of both.

When asked if it works, Hoilman smiles and says, "It just might." Then he climbs in the left front door, turns the key, and smiles even more when a throaty roar drowns out the creaking crickets and burbling creek.

Walking back to the business end of the contraption, he leans his crutch up against the side, takes a small log from his grandson Roy, lays it on the carrier of his saw, then raises it into the whirling blade which quickly and neatly lops off a stove-size chunk.

After demonstrating the efficiency of his machine a few more times, he comes over to enlighten the ignorant.

"I used a '68 Chevrolet car. Three years ago I built this one. I guess I'd built them before. I build one and trade it. Somebody sees it and wants it," he says, a hint of a smile hovering around his lips.

You see, Wes Hoilman is a horse trader, and that sort of thing gets in your blood. You get something that somebody else might want; well, you just have to accommodate him.

The mechanism is extremely simple.

The front of the Chevrolet looks just like the front of a Chevrolet, but the back has been cut down to make room for an axle with two heavy friction pads that rest on the rear tires. When the tires begin to spin, the friction turns the axle that runs through the center of the blade.

Boards nailed to supports keep anyone from accidentally brushing against the spinning tires, and a board carrier with a handle makes putting the wood into the blade safe.

"I seen one made one time. I looked it over real well and decided it wouldn't work. It was made on only one wheel. So I got me a pickup truck, took off the bed, and put me an axle in it and went to sawing," he says.

"I've built several since then," he adds, modestly stirring the dust with his lone crutch.

He has a bum leg that he injured gathering wood.

"I broke it hauling wood out of the mountains with a horse in '70 something or other. The snow was about 6 inches deep, and the horse caught on a big limb. It pulled way back. When it broke loose, it swung around and got my leg.

"It was busted all to pieces,"says Hoilman.

So he uses his sawmill to make life a little easier.

"I use it a lot. Why, I have a power saw, too. I use it in the woods. I haul wood down in my '73 jeep and cut the small ones on my mill," he says.

With a little help from grandson Roy and his machine, Wes Hoilman will make it through another winter with wood to warm him and cook his food.

If you just have to have his sawmill, though, Hoilman will probably make the sacrifice. He lives up a dirt lane about a mile off Double Island Road. After you drive through the creek, begin to look for a Chevrolet sawmill.

Bring cash.

Wes with his Chevrolet sawmill.

Soaring Hawk

HAWKS AND EAGLES

There is power and beauty in the flight of hawks and eagles, a swooping grandeur that stirs the heart. We Americans have chosen an eagle as our national emblem for this reason; we're a proud and independent people represented by a proud and independent bird. While the image of ourselves that we hold continues to shape our national character, the source of that image is often hunted and driven from the skies for no good reason.

When the first white settlers arrived in the southern mountains, there were few valleys that were not patrolled by winged predators, and few rocky faces without their falcons or eagles. For untold centuries these raptors had only themselves to fear, and even the native Americans harmed very few of them. However, with the advent of the white man, these birds found themselves attacked with unreasoning fury.

Bringing with them from their homelands in the British isles a stubborn prejudice against all birds of prey, the early settlers rapidly decimated the population. Tales of chicken, sheep and even small children being carried off justified this slaughter. "Chicken Hawk" became a generic name for any large bird that hovered. While many barnyard fowls made meals for the hawks and their kin, all birds of prey suffered from the wrath of the hardworking farmers and the trigger-happy hunters.

And more recently, their descendants further drove these birds from the skies through the use of DDT and other pesticides which weakened the vitality of the hawks and reduced the strength of their eggs.

For many years the Southern Appalachian skies held few of these raptors—birds with curved beaks and killing claws. Eagles and falcons were virtually gone, and the occasional hawks that flew above the valleys were as likely to be shot as to be admired.

Today, through the efforts of many and growing enlightenment, the noble raptors are once again being seen hovering over mountain balds and shearing through the valley mists.

Danger still lurks in the barrels of guns wielded by the ignorant and the prejudiced, and cars and electric wires take their toll, while pesticides continue to deplete the vigor of the birds.

But raptor populations are growing in the few areas that maintain enough wilderness to provide a refuge. Where the space and the habitat exist, hawks and eagles can flourish. A strong argument against increased development of ridgetops and mountain balds is that these areas once again support significant populations of wildlife of all forms.

In Western North Carolina, efforts to reintroduce the Peregrine Falcon have been rewarded by the number of successful nestings in recent years. In 1990, the vitality of several species renewed hopes for the raptor populations, but especially rewarding was the sight of these falcons who had disappeared from the mountains for several years.

"We have five nesting attempts this year that we've found. Four have been successful, and ten chicks have been produced," said Allan Boynton, mountain project leader for the North Carolina Wildlife Resources Commission.

Over the past several years both North Carolina and Tennessee have participated in hacking programs to reintroduce the falcon.

"Hacking is an old falconry term. It simply means to take a young bird and feed it at a certain place until it learns to fly on its own and to catch its own food. From 1984 through last year we released Peregrines," said Bill Yambert, non-game biologist for the Tennessee Wildlife Resources Agency.

Tennessee's program has not had the success of North Carolina's, although some of the nesting pairs in Western North Carolina may have members hacked by the neighboring state. The birds know no man-determined boundaries, and the number of birds released in adjacent states increases the odds of survival.

"We are well on our way to establishing a falcon population here in the southern mountains," said Boynton.

Another type of raptor seen in the mountains with increasing frequency is the accipiter: hawks that feed largely on birds. Cooper's Hawks and Sharpshins are in the accipiter family.

These hawks usually are seen under or just above the forest canopy, darting rapidly. They have fairly broad wings and long tails.

"The Cooper's Hawk was designated as of special concern—a species in need of monitoring. It was affected by DDT, but is on the road to recovery on its own," said Boynton.

For the past few years, a pair of Cooper's Hawks have had a nest site near Iron Mountain Gap on the Tennessee-North Carolina border. I have often seen these birds flying through nearby coves and just over the forest looking for prey in their established territories.

A more familiar hawk is the buteo. These are the soaring hawks that mostly feed on mammals. Because they expose themselves by their open manner of hunting, they are frequently victims of shootings.

Mountain buteos are the Red-Tailed Hawk, the Red-Shouldered Hawk, and the Broad Wing. The most common is the Red-Tailed Hawk.

A soaring Red-Tail is a frequent sight in the mountains today, for this hawk is making a strong comeback. It is our most common hawk, whose fierce, fighting temperament provides an edge for survival.

Red-Tailed hawk with chick in nest

This past summer two pairs of Red-Tails successfully reared young near Roan Mountain. One pair nested in a steep cove under Eagle Cliffs. With their large nest that had been used before securely established in the top of a towering cherry tree that overlooked all of Buladean, the pair reared a young female. For weeks after she left the nest, the hawk could be found flying about in the neighborhood followed by screaming blue jays.

About five miles away as the hawk flies, another pair raised a young male near Iron Mountain Gap. A tall poplar overlooking a mountain farm and facing the Roan held the nest, a small one that was probably built this year. The attentive parents kept the youngster well supplied with ground squirrels and other small mammals even after he left the nest.

Another generation of Red-Tails has survived the critical first months of existence.

Yet there is little protection against guns, for although illegal, the shooting of Red-Tails is frequent. They are highly visible and often blamed for the depredations of others. Hunters and farmers often take out on these birds their anger against any hawk.

Fortunately, their beauty is one call on human protection.

"A neighbor shot a red-tailed hawk one day. He told me that when he went to pick it up, it was still alive. The longer he looked at it, the prettier it got. He felt real bad about shooting it," said one lifetime resident of the mountains.

"So he took it down by a branch where it could get fresh water and came to feed it every day. Soon it recovered and flew off. He'll never shoot another one," he said.

In addition to the hawks, eagles have been seen in increasing numbers in the mountains. While there is no official record of their nesting, Golden Eagles patrol the southern mountains.

Several times this summer I have seen Golden Eagles between the Roan and Beauty Spot, as well as over the Black Mountains, marvelling as their golden shoulders catch the sun to flash their identities. Increasing sightings are reported throughout the mountains.

Bald Eagles are also seen in the mountains. Pam Scarborough, a naturalist who specializes in birds of prey, has seen one at Doughton Park in Western North Carolina, and I have seen one flying above the Toe River between Mitchell and Yancey Counties and one perched on a high snag at dusk in the same area.

"I think things are improving in the mountains. I see more hawks today than I've seen over the 15 to 16 years I've watched them here. But they are still in danger," said Scarborough.

Red-Tailed hawk fledgling

"While pesticides are still a problem, shooting is also a big problem in some sections. It has to do with the culture. The Scotch-Irish brought the attitude with them that the only good hawk is a dead one. That is gradually changing," said Boynton.

According to an Avery County, North Carolina, grouse hunter, his fellow hunters are serious threats to the hawks and eagles.

"Whenever we are out hunting and they see a hawk, they say, 'Get down, so it won't see us and we can shoot it.' They shoot any one they can, because they blame the hawks for killing grouse. I try to discourage them. but they won't listen to me," he said.

"It is against the law to shoot any hawk; in fact all migratory birds are protected by law," said Scarborough.

"A lot of people will shoot a hawk simply because it is the biggest thing they've seen all day. Also some farmers still think hawks are bad.

"That's a misconception. Actually hawks are beneficial to farmers. It's estimated that each bird saves farmers $1.70 in crop damage by feeding on rodents. That doesn't sound like much, but multiply that by millions of hawks in the world, and you see what a savings it is," she said.

Slowly, attitudes are changing towards the use of pesticides and the unthinking slaughter of birds of prey. The rate of these changes can be loosely gauged by the number of hawks, falcons, and eagles seen in and above our mountain forests and farms.

These living symbols of freedom should be allowed to soar our skies without fear of man.

OLD WAYS

Each year as the fullness of August ripens mountain gardens, fields, orchards, and tobacco patches, the age-old work of the harvest begins.

However, while the same beans, tomatoes, squash, and corn are gathered from today's gardens, the harvest is vastly different from that of 50 years ago. Life on the farms of Western North Carolina and East Tennessee has changed greatly during this century.

In the past, subsistence farming kept many generations together on the land. Each family farm produced most of the food and livestock feed that it needed to survive the long winter months.

"We'd have to buy coffee, salt, sugar, and flour," remembers Howard Burleson, lifelong resident along Greasy Creek in the Buladean community. "Everything else we raised ourselves."

And even some of these store-bought necessities could be obtained from other area farmers.

"A lot of people grew their own wheat and took it to the grist mills on the creeks," he recalls. "There was a mill at Jess Sheets' place. You can still see where it sat."

Even "sweetening" could be found on the farm or in the woods. Honey from farm hives, molasses from sorghum, and syrup from sugar maples substituted for cane sugar during hard times or as a matter of taste.

Today tobacco fields and family vegetable gardens are common; in the first half of the century large fields of corn were raised on every farm to provide feed for horses, cattle, hogs, and other animals.

Also, abundant pastureland provided summer forage and winter hay.

"You should have seen this valley back in the '30s," Burleson says. "Pasture and fields ran right to the top of the ridges."

Today in many places timber has replaced the rows of corn and deep mountain pastures. Rusting barbed wire fences strung along still-solid locusts posts run through the middle of thick woods, reminders of the way things were.

Gathering the hay, as important then as now, took different skills.

Hay mowing machines and hay rakes were horse-powered, the animals helping to gather their own feed. Unlike today's neat, rectangular bales of hay, yesterday's stacks were works of art.

"I started in helping my daddy when I was only this tall," recalls Paul Street, holding his hand waist-high. "He'd haul up the hay and put it down, then I'd stomp around in a circle on it, packing it tight.

"Hay'd keep good as any if you built the stack right," he says. "Pack it down tight, slope the sides like this," (his hands formed a tent) "and you didn't need no covering."

Like tractors and balers, electricity came late to many mountain communities.

Spring houses cooled the dairy products and eggs. Smoke houses cured the meat from the hogs slaughtered along the swift-flowing branches on the first cold days of autumn.

Apple houses kept the bushels of fruit gathered from each farm's trees.

Root cellars kept piles of potatoes, winter squash, candy roasters, and rows of home-canned goods.

Cabbages buried in the fields during harvest kept fresh until dug up from the frozen ground in winter.

Hot peppers were strung up and hung to dry, as were "leather britches," beans in their shells.

"We called them shuck beans, dried beans, or leather britches," Mary Burleson remembers. "We'd string 'em up to dry, then put 'em in a sack with holes so's they could get air."

Household necessities other than food were also home-produced— soap, for example.

"We'd render real fat meat, cooking it down in a brass kettle," Mrs. Burleson says. "We'd strain it to be just as white as snow, then add red devil lye. Three kettlefulls would last us all year."

Cash didn't come easy when outside jobs were scarce or nonexistent.

"My daddy used to hitch the team to our wagon, and we'd go all the way to Johnson City to peddle our potatoes, apples—whatever we had more of than we'd use," Street remembers. "We'd go right over through Greasy Creek Gap, come out at Tiger Creek, then go through Elizabethton to Johnson City."

"We'd be there three days or so, peddling, then buying coffee and whatever else we needed," he says, his mind wistfully traveling those rutted trails and roads again.

"I stayed on my daddy's farm 'til I was 25, timbering and farming and helping. I did better there than going out to work," Street says.

Gradually over the years things have changed. Few mountain farms are what they were, and most mountain counties spend more on their industrial recruiting than on retaining an agricultural base.

"My boys could never go back and live the way we did because they just don't know how. I learned to do for myself and could do it still, but those times are past," Burleson says.

In today's society a weekly paycheck and guaranteed benefits provide the security that 40 acres and a loyal family used to bring.

But the old ways continue to live in the hearts and minds and still-strong backs of an older generation.

SHEPHERD M. DUGGER

BANNER ELK, N.C.—From this high valley in the mountains of Avery County came The Bard of Ottaray (the Indian name for the mountains of Western North Carolina) who captured in resounding prose the life of his homeland.

Shepherd M. Dugger was born in the time of one-room log cabins, primeval wilderness filled with panther, bear, deer and other wildlife, and complete self-sufficiency. He lived to see the automobile roaring over old ox trails and fashionable men and women tripping daintily along paths tread not long before solely by the heavy brogans of native hunters.

Dugger's varied experience during this tumultuous time makes him an ideal spokesman for the people of Ottaray. He was a teacher, school superintendent, hotel proprietor, guide, mining engineer, road builder, farmer, tourism promotor, public speaker and, most importantly, author.

Born in Johnson County, Tennessee, in 1854, Dugger moved with his family to Banner Elk in his early infancy. He experienced the turmoil of the Civil War, the difficult years of reconciliation, the peaceful rural life, the coming of those who wanted to exploit the natural wealth of the mountains, and the advent of the tourist.

With a pen dipped deep in the purplest of inks, he captured these times in high-flown prose. His two books, **The Balsam Groves of the Grandfather Mountain** and **War Trails of the Blue Ridge**, record a time that is gone forever. As more and more development buries even the vestiges of that life, his works assume a greater importance.

The author was keenly aware of the changes that were coming to his beloved homeland. In the first chapter of his first book he says of the mountains:

"Through their mystic veils they whispered an inaudible message of brotherhood to man which none can understand save those who have enjoyed their company in hours of solitude. But the death knell of the sacred oak had been sounded; war between man and the forces of Nature had already begun, and the first battle had been won by the keen-edged axe."

He struggled, trapped in the cleft between using his eloquent pen to celebrate the wonders of his natural heritage and to promote them for the very kinds of development that would destroy them.

The wellspring of his eloquence was Presnell College in Jonesborough, which, he writes, "was then, and I hope is still, the most courtly town in Tennessee, and there I learned a politeness and a courtesy that might justly put to shame all the automobile civilization of the twentieth century." There he became fast friends in the debating club with Robert L. Taylor, later to be congressman, governor, and senator, whose high-flown speeches are as extravagant as Dugger's prose.

Next Dugger attended the University of North Carolina at Chapel Hill where "Bombastical, self-conceited, sap-sucker-headed older students thought it grand to fresh a Mountaineer." A speech in which he attacked his fellow students did nothing to ensure his popularity:

"I am sorry to know that some of you constantly buy whiskey of bootleggers who slip stealthily into the campus at night, and under its influence you thunder through the campus and up and down stairways so much like the shocks of an earthquake that those who would study and rest cannot."

In 1892 his first book was published. **The Balsam Groves of the Grandfather Mountain** inspired some bemused reviews.

The **New York Sun** reviewer stated, "Sweet odors rain from it. Aromatic gales rustle in its branches. The fly leaves are a sovereign plaster for wounds, bruises, and blisters. . ."

The **Ladies' Home Journal** stated that the book was "unique, in that it may be said to have no predecessor and probably it will be without a successor."

Along with the romance of the title, Dugger included information relating to the section and its hotels, a vocabulary of Indian names, a list of altitudes of important mountains and places, Vance's account of the finding of Mitchell's body, and extracts of the journal of Andre Michaux.

The contents of the volume are like the contents of one of Dugger's sentences—there is plenty there, more than plenty, and sometimes too much. His description of the romance's heroine speaks for itself:

"Her raven black hair, copious both in length and volume and figured like a deep river rippled by the wind, was parted in the center and combed smoothly down, ornamenting her pink temples with a flowing tracery that passed round its modillion windings on a graceful crown. Her mouth was set with pearls, adorned with elastic rubies and tuned with minstrel lays, while her nose gracefully concealed its own umbrage, and her eyes imparted a radiant glow to the azure of the sky."

Yet all of the book is not such euphuistic bombast. The depiction of the people of the mountains and their ways is clear and accurate. His discussions of the natural history of the area are precise and informative. His re-creation of the natives' speech is easy to read and captures the sound and sense well.

The main part of the romance takes place on a hike up Grandfather Mountain along a trail that is still in existence. Now called the Shanty

Spring Trail, the path winds past some of the most spectacular of the mountain's many beauties, which form the backdrop for the action of the romantic tale.

For many years Dugger's pen was idle, not because of a lack of desire, but because "The mother of my two sons died when they were very young, and I devoted some twelve of my best years to them." His many and varied occupations supported him and his sons during this period.

His next book was not published until 1932. **War Trails of the Blue Ridge** re-creates the story of the Overmountain Men and their victory at King's Mountain, tells of the Civil War skirmishes in the mountains, and contains several short stories of mountain life. Excepting "John Kite's Log-Rolling," about the book Dugger writes:

"In all the other stories I was a leading or secondary actor and however strange they may appear, they are true with the exception that in 'Lizzie Tuttle,' Jessie did not get dragged off his horse in the mud."

The life of the mountains before "civilization" arrived appears to the reader vividly in this, as in his previous book.

While Dugger's works were out of print for many years, today they are available from the Puddingstone Press, Lees-McRae College, P.O. Box 67, Banner Elk, North Carolina 28604. They are priced very reasonably and well worth the money.

"I doubt if we will ever let them go out of print," says Richard Jackson of Lees-McRae. "We've had orders from all over the place, as far away as California. What made Dugger unique was that he wrote it down, but his knowledge and skill were common to a lot of mountain folks."

While Shepherd M. Dugger died in 1938, you can still come to know him through his books, and he is a good man to know. If you have any interest in the mountains and their past, in the life from Jonesborough to Grandfather Mountain and beyond at the turn of the century, then you will enjoy his books.

MOLASSES

BULADEAN, N.C.—The trip up Pine Root Creek Road last weekend was like a trip to the 1930s. In a clearing on the side of Roan Mountain, a Belgian mare slowly turned an old-fashioned mill, into which a man fed freshly cut cane stalks.

It recalled a time, not so long ago, when mountain families were almost entirely self-sufficient.

"What we couldn't raise or make we learned to live without," remembered Dewey Ingram, Jr., 63, of Buladean.

Over the weekend Ingram brought out his decades-old cane press to revive a community tradition—molasses making. Ingram, along with Geneva Hughes, 83, also of Buladean, and Mrs. Hughes's grandson, Grady Thomas, had decided this was the year to get back into it.

"We used to make cane, me and my husband, but since he died I haven't made any—that was years ago. Then this winter my grandson, he said, 'Granny, when you die they won't be anybody knows how to make molasses,' so this year he put out a patch of cane and now we've got it this far," Mrs. Hughes said as she poured the raw cane juice into an 80 gallon vat.

Just as it must have happened in the early 1900s, a handful of people from the community wandered up Pine Root Creek to help with the molasses making. Friends and relatives took up the jobs that needed to be done, topping the cane, feeding it into the mill, then later stoking the fire and skimming the molasses.

However, there were some jobs that only Granny did. Besides overseeing and directing all of the other activities, she personally strained the raw cane juice through a cloth bag before emptying it into the boiler, and in the end she gave the word when it was time to take the molasses off the furnace.

"Ever since I was a little girl, ever since I was big enough to pull the blades off the cane, I've been making molasses. There wasn't much sugar to buy. We put molasses in everything to sweeten it. We used to make apple butter and pumpkin butter with it," Granny recalled.

Granny's knowledge of molasses was obviously respected by all. When she spoke about the molasses-making process everyone listened carefully.

Even Ingram, who had grown up making molasses, needed to learn what Granny knows.

"This is my first year in a long time. Back in the '40s we made it every year, but I always did that part over there," motioning toward the horse and mill, "I never had no part in the cooking of it. Back then we'd make 30-40 gallons. You didn't sell any of it then. Everybody just made it to use it," Ingram said.

To be appropriately impressed with the fact that they made 30-40 gallons of molasses per family "back then", you must first understand that it takes about twelve gallons of cane juice to make one gallon of molasses. One Saturday they began to mill cane stalks before 9:00 a.m. By noon over 60 gallons of juice was put over an outdoor furnace to boil. It wasn't until 6:00 p.m. that Granny began to pour molasses into clean canning jars.

The entire day's work netted between 5½ and 6 gallons of molasses.

"This work's more for the fun than it is the profit of it. At five dollars a quart they ain't no profit in it," Ingram said.

Watching the entire process of molasses making is fascinating. The truck rolls up loaded with long, thin cane stalks which are topped and then fed through the mill. A large, Belgian mare slowly circles the mill with no encouragement other than an occassional "gi' up, there" from one of the people feeding the mill.

Ingram's mill was built by a local blacksmith nearly 50 years ago. "It don't have a nail in it. We ground on this mill back in the '40s," he said.

Surprisingly, the cane juice that comes out of the mill is a pale green, nothing like the almost black molasses that will be poured into jars at the end of the day.

"It darkens as it boils. At first you just keep them old green skimmings off of it while it boils, then when it cooks down somebody skims while somebody stirs. It don't burn," Granny explained.

After most of the liquid has boiled off or been skimmed off, the vat is carefully lifted with two iron bars and set on the ground. The molasses is strained a final time and then carefully ladled into individual jars.

"That's strained four times before it's put up," Granny said proudly as she watched three strong men carrying the molasses vat.

The final straining has to be done carefully because the liquid is still very hot. On Saturday one man held the heavy cloth sack, filled with the boiling liquid, while two other men squeegeed the molasses down with two cane stalks pinched at either end.

While the favorite way to use molasses is right from the jar over hot, buttered biscuits, it is also tasty in recipes. When measuring molasses, first rinse the spoon or cup with warm water and pour the molasses rather than dipping into the jar. It can be substituted for honey, corn syrup, or sugar.

According to **The Joy Of Cooking**, by Irma S. Rombauer and Marion

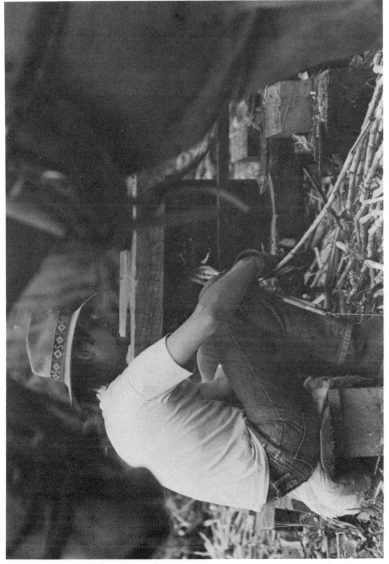

Grady Thomas feeds cane into the mill.

Rombauer Becker, "since molasses is not so sweet as sugar, use 1 cup molasses for ¾ cup granulated sugar. The molasses should replace no more than ½ the amount of sugar called for ...add ½ teaspoon baking soda for each cup molasses called for ...reduce other liquid in the recipe by 5 tablespoons for each cup of molasses used."

GRANNY HUGHES'S GINGERBREAD

1 cup molasses
3 cups self-rising flour
½ cup milk
½ cup butter
2 eggs
1-2 teaspoons ground ginger

Mix and bake in a greased pan at 350 degrees for about 40 minutes or until done.

MARY BARNETT BURLESON'S MOTHER'S MOLASSES CANDY

3 cups molasses
2½ tablespoons butter

My mother would bring the molasses to a boil and let 'em roll for a while until it would spin a hair*. Then she'd take 'em off and add the butter and keep stirring it until it got just warm. Then she'd go to working it with her hands. As it got harder she'd start to pull it, then we'd break off pieces and twist 'em up then lay them out to get hard.

* approximately 238 degrees

RAISIN MOLASSES PIE

from **The Joy of Cooking**, by Irma Rombauer, 1946 edition
Line a pan with an unbaked piecrust.

1¼ cups seeded raisins
½ cup sugar
½ cup molasses
½ cup water
⅛ teaspoon salt
4 tablespoons flour
3 tablespoons water

Stir well, then cook for 15 min. in a double boiler, stirring occasionally, raisins, sugar, molasses, ½ cup water, salt. Combine, then stir in flour, 3 tablespoons water. Cook 15 minutes more. Cool slightly.

Boiling down and skimming the molasses.

Fill pie shell. Bake in 450 degree oven for 10 minutes, then reduce heat to 350 degrees and bake ½ hour longer.

FRIED BANANAS WITH MOLASSES (serves 4)

4 ripe-but-firm bananas, quartered
2 tablespoons butter or olive oil
molasses

Heat oil. Place bananas in oil and fry 3-5 minutes, turning once. While still in the pan, dribble ½ teaspoon molasses over each banana quarter. Serve immediately alone or with two teaspoons sour cream per serving.

The best part of the day is scraping the bottom of the pan.

APPLE BUTTER

BULADEAN, N.C.—As motorists drove along highway 226 one fall weekend, their attention was drawn to a warming scene down by the creek. Four large, steaming cauldrons were the focus of activity for about 30 people—some stirring with long, wooden, L-shaped paddles, some stoking the fires underneath the pots, some tasting, and some giving advice.

The members of the Odom's Chapel Freewill Baptist Church were turning to the past to raise money for their future fellowship hall. They were making apple butter which they will sell for $4 per quart, all proceeds going toward the new building.

"We're putting the roof on today," explained Tillman Arrowood, 72, one of the oldest members of Odom's Chapel.

"Everyone is donating their time. The men here are putting the roof on before the weather turns bad and the others down at the apple butter making are trying to raise money to help finish the building. Our congregation is very generous, for the most part." Arrowood said.

Not only was time and effort being donated, so were all of the ingredients which went into the apple butter. Each family brought sugar, cans and lids, and the apples were donated by two nearby orchards.

"We started out with fifteen or sixteen bushels of apples—stamens and golden delicious, over 170 pounds of sugar, and some cinnamon. I expect we'll end up with nearly 200 quarts, if we're lucky," explained Madeline Campbell.

The apples were stirred constantly, everyone taking turns until the sauce became smooth. The sugar was then added—45 pounds to the larger cauldrons which hold approximately 10 gallons, 40 pounds to the smaller cauldrons. It took lots of hard work and a large quantity of each ingredient, but at the end of the day 163 quart jars were filled with the sweet, cinnamony butter.

"Law, yeah, it was worth it. It was worth it just to bring everyone together like this. Why, used to people'd come together for bean stringin's, quilt makin's, apple butter. Just nobody has time anymore," remembered Geneva Hughes, 83, also a member of the church.

Arrowood said that people had been donating their time and effort to improve the church since he was a young man.

"This is the same structure that was built here when I was about twenty-year-old. Since then it's been bricked, added on to, we just finished the basement, and now we're working on the fellowship hall. Our pastor, Ricky Pate from Johnson City, he's a real good carpenter," he said.

Stella Street stirs apple butter.

The hall is expected to be used for association meetings, conferences, family reunions, and wedding receptions. Nobody had a guess as to when it might be completed.

"We don't have near enough money," Arrowood said, but added that he has faith that somehow the funds will be raised and the building finished.

THE THOMAS WOLFE FESTIVAL
AND MEMORIAL

ASHEVILLE, N.C.—On October 3, 1900, Thomas Wolfe was born in Asheville, North Carolina. Beginning in 1990, his hometown has celebrated the birthday of the acclaimed novelist with the annual Thomas Wolfe Festival.

Centering on the Thomas Wolfe Memorial, from Wednesday through Sunday a variety of events honor Wolfe, who made his city famous (or in the minds of some old-time Ashevillians, infamous).

The Thomas Wolfe Memorial is the rambling old boardinghouse run by his Mother during Wolfe's adolescence and manhood. Depicted as "Dixieland" in his novel **Look Homeward, Angel**, the Old Kentucky Home, as his mother called her establishment, holds shadowy ghosts of the past as well as physical reminders of the life in the turbulent Wolfe house.

Readers of the novel experience a strange sense of déjà vu as they cross the porch to enter the gabled building. Wolfe's detailed descriptions come alive as you walk through the long hall to peer at the period pieces that decorate the 29 rooms; many items that the family used are arranged as they were early in the century.

One small table is covered with the stonecutter's tools that the great gnarled hands of Tom's father, W. O. Wolfe, wielded to provide a living for his family.

In one bedroom are the typewriter and furnishings of Tom's apartment in New York, where he waged a lonely struggle to capture on paper his memories of an at times baffling life in the uproar of the old boardinghouse. His scattered books tell of the scholar's pursuits, while his boat-sized shoes recall the gargantuan figure that strode through the life-filled streets of New York.

The shadowy kitchen holds the large black coal stove and the more modern gas range that his mother Eliza cooked upon to provide the boarders and her family meals. A long, well-used wooden table still holds the bowls and other utensils she and her overworked help handled.

A small border of colored glass windows gives a tinted cast to the light streaming through the larger clear glass into the room where Tom's brother Ben died in October, 1918, a room Tom never again entered.

From the upstairs porch where Tom often slept you can peer through the window at the narrow leap that he made to the window ledge of his first love, Laura in the novel. Below in the yard is the playroom that his father made for Tom and his brothers and sisters.

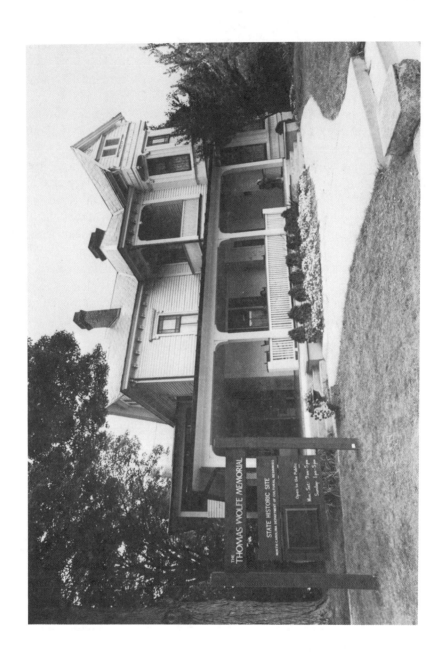

Thomas Wolfe's desk

Kitchen

The guest dining room

Tour group at the house

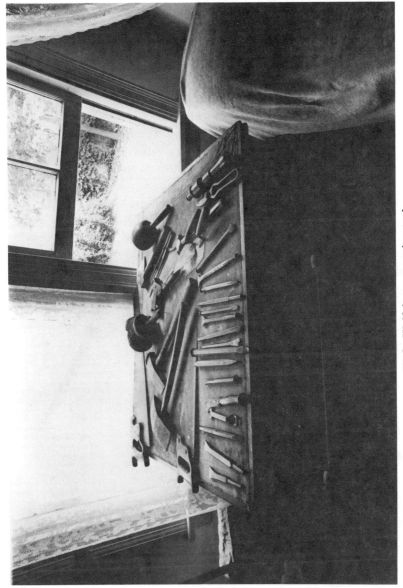

W.O. Wolfe's stonecutting tools

The boarders' dining room holds the several tables where the ever changing men and women sat to dine. Silverware, crockery, and crystal glow in the light entering the large window, and seasonal flowers add color to the clean table settings.

Photographs of various members of the family sit on the mantels and lie upon the walls in several places. And the spirits of these Wolfes seem to lurk right around the many corners.

In 1990 the first Thomas Wolfe festival celebrated his 90th birthday. An Open House at the Thomas Wolfe Memorial began the Festival. Period music in the parlor enlivened the visitors, as well as any lingering ghosts; and refreshments were served, another detail the food-loving Wolfes would have appreciated.

Joining the Wolfe House in celebration was the city of Asheville, which has proclaimed the week Thomas Wolfe Week. Few cities are so identified with a single author as Asheville is with its renowned son.

"Anytime anyone asks me where I was born—it can be New York, Hollywood, London or Paris—when I say Asheville, they all say, 'Wasn't that where Thomas Wolfe was born?' Now what other American author does everyone know the birthplace of?" says John Ehle, a present day Asheville novelist.

Despite the towering new buildings that dwarf the former boarding-house, the streets of Asheville will be familiar to any devotee of the Wolfe novels. And the surrounding mountains remain the same.

For information call (704) 253-8304.

FOLK ART CENTER

ASHEVILLE, N.C.—Every year people from across the country come to Southern Appalachia for the fall colors. Nearly a million travel the scenic Blue Ridge Parkway where the high mountain leaves turn first and most brilliant.

Visitors who travel through Asheville on the parkway are in for an unexpected bonus when they stop at the Folk Art Center located at mile marker 382. Inside are displays of arts and crafts which illustrate the rich handicraft heritage these mountains are famous for.

The Center is itself an Appalachian work of art, made of native wood and stone. Run by the Southern Highlands Handicraft Guild, it houses four galleries, the Allanstand Craft Shop, and a small crafts library. The U.S. Park Service also has an information center and book stand at the entrance of the building.

"Last year half a million people visited us. Some drop in to ask the Park Service about sights on the Parkway and then wander back to the galleries. Some come with this as their destination. Everyone is amazed at the quality of the work on display here," said Lynda McDaniel, public information officer for the Guild.

From gigantic quilts with names like "wedding ring" and "crazy quilt" to wearable fiber art and hand-carved American Indian masks, the galleries display examples of high qualilty works produced by Guild members.

"Not just anyone can become a member. The Guild covers only specific areas and work has to be top-notch," said Ms. McDaniel.

Its members come from the mountain counties of seven states, including Tennessee, North Carolina, and Virginia. Only members whose work passes a rigorous two-part evaluation are allowed into the Guild, she said.

"The members display all sorts of crafts in the galleries. In order to keep things interesting and give more members a chance to show, we change the exhibits regularly. Through October and part of November we will have the work of bookbinding and marbled paper artists Gary Pfaff and Patty Schleicher in the Focus Gallery."

Visitors wander and wonder through the galleries gathering ideas and inspiration for home decorating or a new hobby. "But perhaps the most interesting thing we offer is a program of daily demonstrations," Ms. McDaniel said.

"One day we will have a potter, right in the lobby, answering questions as he shapes a pot. The next we'll have a basket maker weaving while

Inside the Folk Art Center

Visitors examine fine stitches in this quilt in the Members' Exhibit.

Rowena Bradley, traditional Cherokee basketry

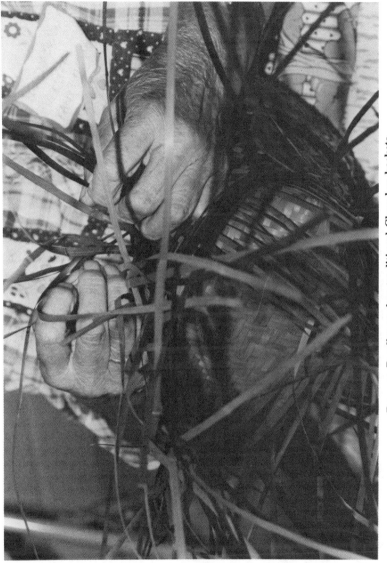

Rowena Bradley makes traditional Cherokee baskets

her partner (and husband) shaves white oak strips to weaving size," Ms. McDaniel explained. "You may even find the basket weaver's materials soaking in the bathroom sink."

In addition to the daily demonstrations, the Guild offers workshops and special programs throughout the year. On October fifth and sixth Betty Kershner will teach silk painting. In November a member will work with other members and the public, teaching each participant to make wooden boxes.

On September 7, about 20 Guild members gathered at the Center for "Celebrate Folk Art." Craftsmen and women demonstrated their skills and peddled their wares to the large crowd that had come in off the parkway. Storytellers enchanted old and young alike from the stage in between performances by bluegrass musicians.

"When we have a shindig we go all out," McDaniel said about the excitement.

At the celebration Phyllis Combs held a young child on her lap, guiding the little hands with her own as a doll emerged from dyed cornshucks.

"My mother taught me. She had to do it for her livelihood when we lost my father. For me it is a source of additional income, but more, it is a source of enjoyment. I think of my mom as I shape the dolls. It's going down into the fourth generation now as I teach it to my own granddaughter," Mrs. Combs said.

Cornshuck dolls and wood chrysanthemums, handwoven placemats and stuffed animals, jewelry and blown glass artwork are available in the Allenstand Craftshop on the first floor in the Center. Whether you want to spend fifty cents or three thousand dollars, the craft shop has something to fit your tastes and pocket change.

"We have four retail shops: The Guild Gallery in Bristol, Virginia, Parkway Craft Center in Blowing Rock, North Carolina, Guild Crafts in Asheville, and this one," Ms. McDaniel said.

The Folk Art Center provides broad exposure for Guild members, thus helping to fulfill the purpose of the 60 year old organization.

"The Guild was founded in 1930 to promote and perpetuate vanishing Appalachian crafts. It has certainly done that and will continue to," said Ms. McDaniel proudly.

For more information on the Guild, the Center, or upcoming programs call (704) 928-7928. Admission is free.

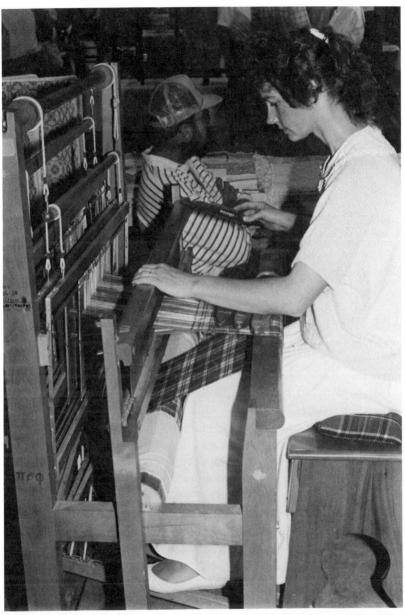

Peggy Whitted weaves a colorful, fine cloth at the "Celebrate the Arts" Festival at the Folk Art Center.

ALVIN OLLIS

BULADEAN, N.C.—Alvin Ollis used to look forward to deer season, cleaning and oiling his guns and soaking his boots in apple juice and acorn scent.

Today Ollis's anticipation of the season is mixed. His duties as owner and proprietor of the Roan View Store often keep him behind the counter when he wants to be behind his rifle.

And to make matters worse, his store is the Big Game Check Station for the area, so he has to watch other hunters bringing in the bucks. In fact, he takes instant photographs of each kill to record on his wall the successes of others.

"Well, it just gives you a heartbroken feeling to see 'em come in when you'd like to be out there with 'em," he said one day as he looked over the photos of kills. "I get so restless that nobody can stand me."

However, Ollis is happy to see that this year already 35 deer have been taken in an area that used to be almost barren of game.

"One of the biggest things that's helped our area is the Tennessee Deer Management Program. Their deer eventually infiltrate our area," he said. Buladean is just on the other side of Iron Mountain from Tennessee, and deer don't respect state lines.

"Since people have begun seeing deer on their places, a lot of them have posted their land, and that's helped the deer population, too," he said.

Another factor in the resurgence of game in the area is the work of the local game warden, Richard Stowe.

"Richard is a good warden," Ollis said. "He is another big reason the deer herd has grown. People know that he'll stay out all night and roam the woods to catch poachers."

A native of the Buladean community, Ollis has watched the ebb and flow of wildlife over the years and has come to appreciate the many difficulties that the animals face in their struggle for survival. He has developed some ideas for increasing the odds in their favor.

A few years ago he tried to interest others in Buladean in a plan to close certain areas of the community for hunting for a few years while a stocking program was introduced.

"I thought that if we could close one side of the road (highway 226 splits Buladean into two nearly equal parts) for five years with a management program, then open that side and close the other, we could get healthy herds in the area with the deer having time to breed," he said.

While many Buladean residents supported the idea when he mentioned it to them, as the time came to agree to implement the plan, most changed their minds.

"Well, they agree with you up to the point you try to take action in that direction, then they back down," Ollis said.

Seeing the deer that are brought in has also made him unhappy with the bag limit of three deer.

"Right now three deer is too much. A lot of people have checked in two or three deer. They know they will have another chance, so they shoot a young one, knowing that they can get a trophy buck later. In some states they got to the point that you're allowed only a buck with four visible points. Gives deer more chance to mature," he said.

Ollis knows what is being harvested in Buladean. Several times an hour he wanders over to the wall to look over the snapshots he has taken to immortalize others' successes. He knows the number of points and the spread of each kill.

At midweek he still had hopes of getting one himself, slim hopes.

"Usually the first three days is when most of the deer is brought in, and I was working all during that time," he said, shoulders drooping.

"I didn't get to hunt until a week or ten days after the season opened. I might have hunted eight or ten hours total. I'm still hoping to get in a few more hours," he said, straightening up with eyes looking through the store walls to isolated coves thick with trophy buck.

"I'm really against just shooting game to say I've killed something. I hate to see people kill doe deer and just leave 'em laying, or shoot their limit in squirrel and feed them to their dogs, or leave an arrow or a bullet in a deer and let it wander off.

"Any animal killed ought to have all its parts used to its fullest extent," he said, his mouth watering at the memory of venison steaks and his eyes wandering to a buck head that oversees the activity in the store.

If you're driving through Buladean, stop in to see the pictures on the wall, but if you have a fresh kill in the back, break it to Alvin gently.

Buchanan Homeplace

HOMECOMING

BULADEAN, N.C.—Homecoming—coming home. It is something that many Americans can do no longer. Mobility and change have spread families and destroyed many old homesites.

The Buchanans of Buladean are more fortunate than most. The foresight of their father, Leonard, planted a seed which has struck deep roots in the family consciousness.

"When my Dad died, he said, 'I want anybody in the family to be able to come back here as long as there is any Buchanan alive'," said Maye Buchanan Tipton on a cool October day when the family had gathered at the homesite.

She looked up the cove into the brilliant fall foilage, then returned her gaze to the old homestead.

"When he was failing, he came back here and went up in the woods and sat on a log and said that. Since then it's always been a family thing to come together here," she said.

Leonard's father, Adam, built the old house in the middle of the nineteenth century, around 1850 or '60. Since then it has stood as solidly in place as the large boulder that juts above the branch that flows beside the cabin.

First the front cabin was built, a one room structure with a fireplace. The original poplar logs still stand firmly in place, though the chinking has leaked out here and there.

"Those are dove-tail joints. The logs were put up green, then shrunk in tight. Each has a locust plug in an auger hole. They were hewed with a broadaxe and a foot adze, then chinked with clay," said Max Hopson, one of those gathered to celebrate their heritage.

"They used wormy chestnut to make the shingles with a froe," he added, pointing to the tin roof that has since replaced the native materials.

Later, an upper cabin was added.

"Adam built all this. He built two houses, the upper house and lower house. You had to go outside to get from one to the other. They weren't joined together for a long time, not until the kitchen was built," said Robert Garland, grandson of Adam and nephew of Leonard.

Adam Buchanan was one of the first settlers up Bean's Creek in Buladean. He arrived when the only way in was a rough sled road. He founded his family in the independent, self-sufficient style of the traditional mountaineer.

He raised hogs, cattle and poultry. He grew a garden for the family and corn for the livestock. He also ran a water-powered grist mill about a mile and a half below the home.

Dovetail Joint

Six of Leonard Buchanan's children, left to right: Rath, Albert, J. Henry, Nancy, Maye, Irene.

"Certain days were mill days. Everyone that could carry a peck, they would load them up. That would be a holiday for the children. They would all get together to play," Robert said.

Up until he was five years old, Robert was raised by his grandfather Adam and his grandmother Nancy, for his mother had to take work in Erwin. He remembers those distant days still.

"My grandpap had a sheep he kept with his milk cows. A sheep will come home every night. Those cows would follow the sheep home. You didn't have to go into the mountains to get them to milk of an evening," he said.

Leonard and his wife Margaret moved in with his parents when ill health struck Adam.

"He took heart dropsy and swelled all over. He was homebound for several years before he went," said Robert, who was there and remembers well.

He also remembers the death of the patriarch.

"He went to Bakersville for the elections. He had to ride horseback over there. There was a big boarding house—so much for bed and board and to feed the horse."

Election returns were slow in coming. So Adam waited three or four days for Western Union to wire the results. He rode back to Bean's Creek to tell the settlement what had happened.

He was worn out. His own bed felt good.

"Me and my grandpap and my grandmaw slept up in the upper house. My grandmaw got up and came out to help Aunt Margaret. Then she came back to help him dress, but he didn't answer.

"He had died with me asleeping right with him," said Robert.

Life with the next generation continued to the rhythm established by Adam: farming, raising stock, growing apples, gathering chestnuts, and peddling the excess products of their life over the mountain in Tennessee.

"Life was pretty tough in here, but we were tough, too," said Albert Buchanan, one of Leonard and Margaret's 13 children born from 1911 to 1938.

The children attended a one room school house right across the road from their homestead. The building still stands, though it has been turned into a vacation home by some people from Charlotte.

It also served as the church house.

"We didn't have electricity up here until I was in high school. We used oil lamps and had a battery powered radio. We had an outside antenna that ran way up to the top of the ridge," said Rath Buchanan, Albert's younger brother.

View of Bean's Creek Road from the porch of the cabin.

The "famous rock," a playground for five generations of Buchanan children.

"My mom was real strict. She thought that listening to shows like **Sgt. Preston and Yukon King** and **Fibber McGee** would make us go bad," he said.

The children found fun where it lay. One of the centers of entertainment was and is the large rock by the creek.

"I remember Albert and I fell off the big rock. We came all the way down, into the water. I guess that I cried, but now I can laugh," said Irene Buchanan Henderson, one of the sisters.

Her daughter Judy Reed has also played on the rock, as have her daughters. "The girls like to play on the big rock in Mitchell County, just as their mom did when she was young. We love going to Mitchell County so we can keep in touch with our roots."

Leonard's granddaughter Faye Gold also remembers the rock. "I have so many fond memories of the times we have been at the old house, as children and adults. My favorite is climbing that old rock, of course.

"What a monument that rock has become in our lives! It has provided all of us with a link that is unbreakable and the thought of it makes me warm all over," she said.

At the Homecoming, the rock was seldom empty of children. They scrambled up and over and down. There must be magic or magnetism in it, for none fell.

For the adults there was less energetic entertainment. Albert, his wife Alma, Max, his wife Alice, and Bonnie Byrd sang gospel music. They opened with "The Homecoming," a song about the heavenly homecoming when those sundered by death will be together once more.

Lloyd Buchanan's blessing before the bountiful dinner cooked on the old wood cook stove also sounded the theme of homecoming. He called to mind the grand banquet in heaven where all would be reunited.

The Buchanans ended the day with a ceremonial pressing of apple cider, a sacrament of remembrance of times past and a pledge of times to come. The commitment to preserve the old homeplace unifies the family down through the generations.

Maye Buchanan Tipton sums up the family feeling, "This is home. This is where my roots is."

The family pressed cider at the end of the day.

JOHN EHLE

PENLAND, N.C.—John Ehle has won fame as a novelist and earned contentment in his traditional mountain home. His life and his art intertwine in a way that makes each more wonderful.

Ehle's 110-year-old home lies down a winding dirt road which seems to drop a decade at each turn until reaching the peace and simplicity of the 1880s at his log house above the Toe River.

The notched logs and old stone chimneys nestled among aging apple trees beside a trickling mountain branch evoke the days of homespun clothing and work-hardened hands when each family was largely self-sufficient.

These are the days recreated in many of Ehle's novels.

If ghosts walk through the thick walls or rise from the hardwood floor, they are sure to find themselves between the covers of a book.

"There is a little cemetery up there," Ehle says, pointing to a wooded rise above his house, "filled with the bones of laborers killed while building the Clinchfield and Ohio Railroad through here."

"One of my novels, **The Road**, is about the building of the railroad from Old Fort to Ridgecrest. It was built largely by convict labor. Many died. As many as 400 in one field are buried," he continues. "Now the men buried up here are not the same as those who died along that stretch, but the difficulties and dangers were the same."

Ehle, who was born in Asheville, North Carolina, has made the mountains and their past a part of his life. His novels have the texture of the days they describe; it's a firsthand feeling.

His birthplace is not only the urban center of North Carolina mountain life; it is the home and setting for the state's most famous writer, Thomas Wolfe.

"Anytime anyone asks me where I was born—it can be New York, Hollywood, London or Paris—when I say Asheville, they all say, 'Wasn't that where Thomas Wolfe was born'," says Ehle, good-humored exasperation dancing in his eyes. "Now what other American author does everyone know the birthplace of?

"I hadn't even read Thomas Wolfe when I wrote my earlier novels. My mother said it was a dirty book. She wouldn't let me read it. She loaned **Look Homeward, Angel** to a woman who didn't return it.

"The only thing that interested her was that my Aunt Netty knew all of the people," he says, the good humor turning to a laugh. "Now that I've read him, I admire his work tremendously.

"I was compared to Thomas Wolfe by every reviewer of **Lion on** the Hearth (his first novel set in Asheville). *The New York Herald Tribune* reviewer wrote that I was better than Thomas Wolfe. That might be why they failed,'' he says, again breaking into laughter.

When Ehle started to work on his first novel of mountain life, **The Land Breakers**, he supplemented his firsthand knowledge of his material with research.

"I read everything I could find on the early period. I used index cards. Under 'fall' I'd put anything that people did in the fall,'' says the novelist.

The seasons provided more than a backdrop for the early settlers and farmers in the mountains. Everything moved with the natural cycle, as Ehle's works depict. In fact, he is in the middle of a tetralogy in which each novel is set in a different season. He has already written two parts—**The Journey of August King** and **The Winter People**.

"Those two books are companions. They both take place in a very short time in one season. I had wanted to call the first one **Autumn Procession**, but the publishers didn't like the title—said it sounded like a book on the leaves turning. I'm inclined to agree with them at this point,'' he says.

"I am now working on one I call **Summer Story**,'' adds Ehle. "They all have a kind of tragic element.''

Both **The Journey of August King** and **The Winter People** caught the attention of Hollywood. While **August King** is under option, **The Winter People** was filmed in North Carolina.

Finding the right setting for the film fell to Ehle, who took the moguls on a tour of his selected sites.

"Bill Arnold of the North Carolina film commission and I had scouted out before. I'd taken him to Plumtree because of the old store. He told me, 'John, let's save the best for last. They won't take anything until the end of the day.'

"Since we picked them up in Asheville, we stopped first at Pensacola. We took them all the way back to the fishing lodge; they took a lot of pictures.

"Now, some of it was written with Pensacola in mind. I used to go back to that fishing lodge, but it's awful hard to tell Hollywood people anything. We did the best we could,'' explains Ehle. "The excitement was being held. They didn't want to reveal excitement until they'd seen 'the' place.

"At Plumtree they became little boys running around with their cameras taking pictures. They came out at an average age of about 14,'' says Ehle, breaking into laughter at the memory.

Although the novelist didn't write the screenplay for the movie, he was given a consultancy.

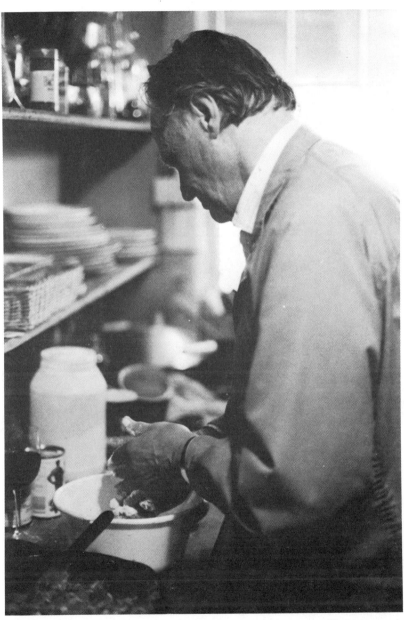

Among his friends John Ehle is *most* famous for his buttermilk biscuits.

"I had the opportunity to comment. They had Collie (the heroine) using God's name in vain. I told them that mountain women wouldn't do such a thing. I'd mention things like that," says Ehle.

"The screenwriter has been quoted as saying that most of the problems an adapter would have was solved in the novel itself," he adds. "I wouldn't let one movie be done because of the distortion of the book."

Such a stand is difficult to take, for the financial rewards from Hollywood are great.

"Funny, it isn't a joy to be a writer, but it is a joy to write. The profession of being a writer is full of pitfalls; it is virtually impossible to make a living as a writer," Ehle says.

"I've had 4 or 5 books taken by book clubs—one does make money out of book clubs. One does make money out of motion pictures, either options or films. Without those I wouldn't have made enough money to make it pay," he says, gesturing towards a line of his books on a nearby shelf.

The books are the only sign of authorship in the old log house. No word processors beep and glow. No dictating machines or busy secretaries break the charm. Ehle writes with a pen on paper, with the sound of the birds outside and the occassional clacking of the train passing along the river to punctuate the breeze in the trees.

To join him in the mountains, pick up one of his novels and enter a world that is passing with each year.

THE BLACK MOUNTAINS

Towering above all the Eastern United States is the Black Mountain range, the special pride of the Southern Appalachians. The beauty of the range can be appreciated from a distance, for every high mountain provides a view of the Blacks on a clear day. But the best way to see Mount Mitchell and its brothers is to drive up to Mount Mitchell State Park, located just off the Blue Ridge Parkway, which runs along the southern edge of the range.

The story of the Black Mountains breaks into two parts. The first part covers over a billion years of their history, the second only a few decades. Yet the latter few years of their history threaten to overweigh and eventually cancel the unthinkable span of time that precedes them.

For the Black Mountains are now dying, being rendered sterile by the noxious poisons of a culture that has lost touch with the true power of the universe and enthroned its short-sighted logic in the place of the millenia proven strength of nature.

BIG TOM WILSON

Many years which have brought revolutionary changes have passed since Thomas D. Wilson, known as Big Tom, dominated the enclosed valley under the Black Mountains, but neither the years nor the changes have diminished the fame of this archetypal mountain man.

Big Tom rose from the obscurity of the shadows of the headwaters of the Cane River when he discovered the body of the famous explorer and scientist, Elisha Mitchell, in 1857. The unerring woodcraft of the simple hunter and farmer enabled him to trace Mitchell's trail from a meadow under the peak later named for the scientist to the pool carved by a waterfall which claimed the explorer's life.

From that time Big Tom, and later his sons and grandsons, became the guide of choice for anyone venturing the ascent of the Blacks from the Pensacola side.

Born in 1825 on the Toe River on the other side of the Black Mountains, Big Tom grew up in the wilderness setting of the Toe River Valley that is bounded by the Blue Ridge, the Roan, the Unakas, and the Black Mountains. Only the native Indians before the coming of the white men had the kind of intimate knowledge of the ways of the wild that came naturally to the boy raised with the woods as his schoolroom, playroom, and food source.

A year after his 1852 marriage to Niagara Ray, who was to bear him

The Black Mountain Range

nine (some say twelve) children (a feat that entitles her to renown also) on their primitive farm, Big Tom moved his family to the headwaters of the Cane River where he achieved his fame and established his clan.

"I remember going to stay at his house when I was young; he wasn't nothing to be afraid of," says Brook Wilson, Big Tom's grandson, who at 92 is a living link to a mythic past. "And he used to come stay all night at our house. I'd go rabbit hunting with him. I wasn't big enough to be carrying a gun. I just went with him for company.

"He was quite a hunter. I believe it was 13 bears he had in his yard one time. He killed 118 bears in his lifetime," says Brook proudly.

While some sources say 113, others 114, none dispute that Big Tom was the greatest bear hunter of the Southern Appalachians and had the greatest number of kills. His sons and grandsons followed (and some of the great and great-great grandsons continue to follow) his hunting ways, though none has ever eclipsed his record.

On the wall of his sitting room, grandson Brook has a photograph of Big Tom with a bear cub on the end of a chain. Brook says:

"He'd take that bear to Asheville and would walk the streets with him. He caught it young and raised it up. He kept it for years."

An Asheville writer, Harold E. Johnston, has described the town's reception of the hero with or without bear:

"Big Tom would generally make two to three visits to Asheville each year, making the journey, twenty-seven miles each way, afoot, and his powerful figure with its massive head, snowy locks and beard, and kindly eyes, attracted great attention as he walked the streets. On such occasions his friends here, and almost the entire population of Asheville claimed the honor of being his friend, from the highest to the lowest vied with each other in doing him honor."

Johnston, who interviewed Big Tom in 1903, also gives the mountain man's own account of his greatest tracking feat—finding and following Mitchell's last trail that was over ten days old:

"I called Bob Patton and the rest of the boys and showed them the footprint on the log, then trailed further, calling as I did so: 'Here boys, here's where he's went!'

"Bob Patton says: 'How can you say "Here's where he's went when you couldn't track a horse here"?' Says I: 'Come here and I'll show you where he's went twenty-five yards ahead.' He says: 'I'll be glad if you'll do so!' I broke a twig off of a laurel bush and showed him both sides of the leaves. Says I: 'The outside of these leaves is dark green, and the inside light green. Now look ahead and see where he's turned up the white side of those laurel leaves breaking his way thro' that thicket.' He slapped me on the shoulders and said: 'Go ahead! You

Big Tom Wilson

are better than any old hound I ever had in these mountains! I'll follow you, let you go where you will.' ''

Big Tom then led his followers down the miles-long trail that ended in the icy waters of a lonely mountain falls. This summer adventure in 1857 began Big Tom's mythic reputation.

David Hunter Strother, a travel writer-illustrator for *HARPER'S NEW MONTHLY MAGAZINE,* had visited the Black Mountains the winter before Mitchell's death. He and his companions were directed to Big Tom as a guide for their ascent of Mount Mitchell. The ''stalwart woodsman leaning on a rifle, and attended by two dogs'' readily agreed.

This illustrated article in a national magazine introduced Big Tom to a wide audience, and the finding of Mitchell's body solidified his fame. From this year no trip to the Black Mountains was complete without a visit to Big Tom Wilson.

In 1885 Charles Dudley Warner, a writer who collaborated with Mark Twain on a novel, traveled the rough road to the Wilson boundary. As he later wrote, ''Big Tom himself weighed in the scale more than Mt. Mitchell, and not to see him was to miss one of the most characteristic productions of the country, the typical backwoodsman, hunter, guide.

''He is six feet and two inches tall, very spare and muscular, with sandy hair, long gray beard, and honest blue eyes. He has a reputation for great strength and endurance; a man of native simplicity and mild manners,'' added Warner, who was amazed at the guide's stories. ''The stream flowed on without a ripple.

''There was an entire absence of braggadocio in Big Tom's talk, but somehow as he went on, his backwoods figure loomed larger and larger in our imagination, and he seemed strangely familiar. At length it came over us where we had met him before. It was in Cooper's novels. He was the Leather-Stocking exactly,'' wrote the traveler.

Although Big Tom died in 1908, his sons and their sons and their sons have continued to live in Yancey County, perpetuating the name and carrying on the traditions of their famous progenitor.

And sharing the crest of the Black Mountains with Mount Mitchell is the nearby peak, Big Tom, formerly one of the Black Brothers. The wilderness-loving native son and the scholarly professor are memorialized by the mountains they loved.

ELISHA MITCHELL

While Big Tom is typical of the larger-than-life heroes, hunters and fighters of the Southern Appalachians, the curious scholar and teacher,

Elisha Mitchell, earned his fame with pen rather than gun and careful research rather than unerring aim.

Born in Connecticut in 1793, Mitchell early showed his talents for scholarship. He graduated from Yale with high honors in 1813 and came to the University of North Carolina to teach in 1818 as professor of mathematics and natural philosophy. He later assumed the chair of chemistry, geology, and mineralogy, while lecturing in Latin, logic, history, geography, and composition.

One of his students, Zebulon B. Vance, wrote, "So great and accurate were his attainments, that he was the referee of all knotty or disputed points which arose in the other departments; and it was said of him that at a moment's notice, in case of absence or sickness, he could fill the chair of any other professor in the university."

Another student, not quite so literate, confided to his diary, "Dr. Mitchell is a very humerous old man, and certainly a man who never spoke without displaying some learning. I am confident I never heard such an entertaining lecture in my life. He brought in every sciance to illustrate some point, and seemed perfectly acquainted with each of them."

However, Mitchell's classroom erudition was only one source of his fame; his pioneering explorations of the mountains of Western North Carolina have given his name to a mountain, the highest in the Eastern United States, and to a county rimmed by the towering masses he studied and measured.

In 1825 he took charge of a geological survey funded by the state of North Carolina. This was the first statewide survey to be undertaken by any of the United States.

During the summers of 1827 and 1828, Mitchell first entered the mountainous counties of the state to further his study. The wonders of this area brought him back several times before the explorations claimed his life in 1857.

In 1828 when he first climbed Grandfather Mountain to see the stirring view from its summit, he observed the higher mountains surrounding it.

"It was a question with us," he wrote, "whether the Black and Roan Mountains were not higher than the Grandfather and we were all inclined to give them the palm."

This question was to dominate Mitchell's life to its end.

In 1835 Mitchell returned to the area prepared for serious experimentation and measurements to fill out his studies of the mountains. In his memorandum book he cursorily noted his intentions and his tools:

"Objects of attention—Geology; Botany; Height of the Mountains; Positions by Trigonometry; Woods, as of Fir, Spruce, Magnolia, Birch;

REV. ELISHA MITCHELL, D.D.

Fish, especially Trout; Springs; Biography, &c. . .tools-Two Barometers, a Quadrant, a Vasculum for plants, and a Hammer for rocks.''

Establishing a base in Morganton, Mitchell proceeded on horseback to explore the Linville Gorge, Table Rock, and Linville Falls, which he descended. Then he climbed Grandfather again to measure its height barometrically, the method he employed throughout this trip.

Next he climbed the Roan, taking its elevation and writing:

"It is the most beautiful and will best repay the labor of ascending it of all our high mountains. With the exception of rocks looking like the ruins of an old castle near its southwestern extremity, the top of Roan may be described as a vast meadow without a tree to obstruct a prospect, where a person may gallop his horse for a mile or two, with Carolina at his feet on one side, and Tennessee on the other, and a green ocean of mountains raised into tremendous billows immediately about him.''

After his work on the Roan, Mitchell traveled to the Black Mountains, where he spent almost a week climbing different peaks to take measurements to ascertain which was the dominant one.

In an article appearing in the *Raleigh Register* in November, 1835, Mitchell described one of these climbs:

"The roughness of the sides and top of Black Mountain is likely to prevent his being often ascended from motives of curiosity and pleasure. A route, very much better than that pursued by us, is not likely to be discovered, and that can be accomplished only on foot; and for between one and two miles, it is thro' thick laurels and along a bear trail . . . which though an excellent kind of turnpike probably in view of the animal that formed it, is much less highly approved by the two legged animal who tries it after him.''

With only his six weeks vacation from the University to utilize for his explorations, Mitchell had to hurry his work, but still he came to the conclusion that ensured his fame and led to his death:

"The Black Mountain [range] . . . has some Peaks of greater elevation than any point that has hitherto been measured in North America, East of the Rocky Mountains.''

In 1835 and again in 1844 Mitchell returned to the Black Mountains to continue his work.

During the latter trip, after a particularly strenuous day of climbing, he wrote his wife, "I could not help thinking as I crawled along over leaves under a shelving rock what a comfortable place it would be to die in.''

His own words foretold his fate.

In the mid-1850s the famous North Carolina politician-mountain climber Thomas L. Clingman published an article in which he disputed Mitchell's claims to have climbed and measured the highest peak of the Black Mountains. A pamphlet war arose that heated tempers and disturbed the academic calm of Professor Mitchell.

Clingman, described by historian Ora Blackmun as "a man whose self-confidence often reached the state of arrogance and one unrelenting in a quarrel," goaded Mitchell into an angry response.

"Do not, sir, issue another foolish and detestable pamphlet. It will do me some injury, but greater mischief to your own character, not only as a politician, but also as a man; especially when I take up the pen, and expose its untruth, its injustice, its weakness, and its wickedness," wrote the gentle Professor.

Mitchell returned to the Black Mountains in 1856 for a short time and in 1857 to measure and explore and to obtain affidavits from his earlier guides to refute Clingman's claims.

On Saturday, June 27, Mitchell left his son Charles at the Mountain House, a refuge for those climbing the Blacks, saying that he was going to descend to the Cane River Valley. After Professor Mitchell failed to return to their meeting place for several days, his son became worried and obtained a guide to take him to the valley.

When they arrived in the settlement, they found that no one had seen the Professor.

On Friday evening, July 3, the search began. Mitchell's former student, Zeb Vance, happened to be visiting in the area and joined the search party. His account of the search was published later.

Saturday's weather was unpropitious—rain, temperatures in the 40's, thick clouds obscuring all.

"It seemed as if the genii of those vast mountain solitudes were angered at our unwonted intrusion, and had evoked the Storm-God to enshroud in deeper gloom the sad and mysterious fate of their noble victim," wrote Vance.

Finally, on July 7, Big Tom Wilson, following faint signs, discovered Mitchell's body in a deep pool under a waterfall which now bears the Professor's name.

Despite the difficulty, several men of the search party carried the body up the steep mountain through the thick laurel to the top.

Although the Mitchell family prevailed over the searchers' wishes to have the Professor buried on the mountain he explored and had the body brought to Asheville for interment, they later acceded to the wishes of the mountaineers and exhumed Elisha Mitchell to be buried on the

Mitchell Falls

highest peak of the Black Mountains, where his grave can still be seen on the summit of the mountain that bears his name.

MOUNT MITCHELL

Today, Elisha Mitchell does not rest easy on the rugged summit of the ancient mountain named in his honor. The thick, dark stands of spruce and fir that gave the Black Mountains their name are dying all around his grave.

Stark silver boles now stand where dark green, living trees once flourished. And little hope exists for the remaining life on the summits of the highest range east of the Mississippi.

Ozone, acid rain, heavy metals, and other industrial pollutants which characterize the civilization of the United States as well as most of the rest of the developed world have so altered the ecology of these peaks that life which has flourished upon them since the last ice age is dying, and reproduction is almost nonexistent.

Until recently, Mount Mitchell's story has been one of natural processes, of gradual change over millions of years.

More than a billion years ago, the buckling of the supercontinent, a large land mass comprising all of the present-day continents, thrust a tremendous mountain range to tower where the Appalachians now stand. Erosion gradually leveled these mountains, the sediments washing into a shallow sea formed by the drifting apart of the supercontinent.

When the continents drifted together again about 600 million years ago, the collision created a new mountain range, the present-day Appalachians, which then towered over three miles high. Subsequent shifts and erosion have brought them to their present stature.

While Mount Mitchell and the other Black Mountains are much diminished in height, they still dominate all of North America east of the Rocky Mountains.

Another natural event has helped to create the unusual environment of the Black Mountains today. The southward march of the glaciers, which brough a climate typical of today's northern Canada to yesterday's South, left traces after their retreat and the return of a warm climate.

The red spruce-Fraser fir forest with its plants and animals typical of alpine Canada exists on the summits of the highest mountains of the Southeast where the climate remains much colder than that of the surrounding lowlands. The Black Mountains have an extensive spruce-fir forest. Unfortunately, it is this forest which is rapidly deteriorating.

Mount Mitchell (left)

A billion years of natural metamorphoses has been interrupted by a relatively few years of man-made pollution.

One of the best ways to see the Black Mountains is walking their slopes. Their history is written on the face of the land.

Huge stumps left from logging earlier in this century, the logging trails, roads, and railway beds, crumbling chimneys and discarded wood stoves, decaying locust fences and the gaping mouths of old mines reveal the hand of man, as the weathered rocks reveal the work of time.

These scars heal quickly in geologic time, becoming part of the patina that proves these mountains ancient.

However, today a far more insidious attack progresses slowly but surely—the invisible poisons, acids, and heavy metals spewed into the atmosphere are settling onto the trees, seeping into their systems and soaking into the soil. Clouds which often envelop the peaks in soft beauty have become poison baths for the mountain growth.

Running roughly south to north, with a fishhook curve at the southern extremity, the Black Mountains form a barrier to clouds moving through from the West, the location of the Tennessee Valley and the Ohio Valley with their constant discharge of noxious emissions from heavy industry. The peaks and the western slopes receive regular doses of these poisons.

For several years the decline of the spruce-fir ecosystems in the Southeastern Applachians has been documented, as has a similar decline in high elevation forests of New York and New England. The Bavarian Forests of West Germany are dying also, with the name *Waldsterben* being coined for the phenomenon.

Finally an organization has undertaken the task of investigating the problem to determine more precisely the causes of the deterioration of the forest.

SARRMC (the Southern Appalachian Research-Resource Management Cooperative) has instituted the Spruce-Fir Ecosystem Assessment Program, which has already gathered data, while planning further research activities covering many different aspects of the problem.

Organized in 1976, SARRMC provides coordinated research, extension, and educational support programs concerning the Southern Appalachians and their resources. Members include the Tennessee Valley Authority, the U.S. Fish and Wildlife Service, the U.S. Forest Service, the National Park Service, Virginia Polytechnic Institute and State University, Western Carolina University, Clemson University, North Carolina State University, the University of Georgia, and the University of Tennessee.

The complexity of the ecosystem and the various man-made environmental changes combine with natural enemies of the spruce-fir forest to create an extraordinarily intricate puzzle for the professors, scientists, and foresters to piece together. The investigators are breaking the puzzle into sections so that they can gain verifiable knowledge of the complex interactions. Such factual data is essential to eventually completing the entire puzzle.

Certain facts have already been clearly established. "Specific features of forest decline include excessive mortality, growth suppression, reproduction failure and absence of seedlings, crown thinning, canopy yellowing and loss of vigor, and reduced capability to resist pests and diseases. . . . Spruce-fir on Mount Mitchell exhibit all of these decline symptoms," according to the research and management operating plan for the SARRMC Spruce-Fir Ecosystem Assessment Program.

Surveys undertaken in 1984 on Mount Mitchell showed "Red Spruce growing at altitudes of 6,350 feet or higher were found to be in a severe state of decline. Trees of age 45 to 85 years average 75-90 percent defoliation. . . . All trees at or above 6,350 feet elevation regardless of vigor exhibit marked growth reduction beginning in the early 1980s.

"On numerous samples, the 21 annual growth increments (trunk rings) from 1962 to 1983 were equivalent in total diameter to the four annual increments of 1958 to 1961," the document continues.

In addition, on west-facing slopes above 6,350 feet, the SARRMC team observed no successful fir, spruce, or shrub reproduction.

"The ground was barren of any living woody vegetation . . . by contrast, a vegetation survey of 1958 showed all Mt. Mitchell slopes from the summit down had lush and abundant ground cover," says the report.

The team also noted extensive root damage and the presence of pathogenic root fungi, as well as high levels of lead deposition.

A resurvey of the same plots in 1985 by Robert Bruck of North Carolina State University revealed that "the percentage of trees exhibiting decline symptomatology" is "significantly higher than that observed in 1984."

He noted an increase in all levels of diseased and dead trees, indicating that while 88 percent of the red spruce were rated as healthy in 1984, only 49 percent remained so in 1985.

SARRMC plans to run several different experiments to test hypotheses attributing damage to acid rain, gaseous pollutants, trace metals, and combinations of pollutants. However, the complexity of the problems rules out early pinpointing of a cause.

"Acid rain and lead constitute only two parts of an incredibly complex ecological perturbation that appears to be taking place exclusively in high altitude regions," stresses Bruck.

Bob Biesterfeldt of the Southeastern Experimental Station adds, "One possible reason that the higher elevations may be more affected is that they are enshrouded in the clouds carrying the toxic substances more often and for longer periods than lower elevations are.''

"Those mountains spend half their lives in the clouds," says Timothy Crawford of the TVA, adding, "The process by which clouds incorporate, transform, and transport pollutants are currently poorly understood."

The problem is clear. Acres and acres of dead and dying trees have transformed the Black Mountains into silver-streaked ones, and other high elevation forests are suffering the same decline.

The solution is not so clear. Even if the scientific studies eventually provide a precise cause-and-effect explanation, will the industries and the consumptive lifestyles of this and other countries retrench and adjust to prevent emissions that carry death with them as they float above the lowlands to anchor on the mountains?

And what of the life that lies beneath these mountains? Where do the poisons go as they fall from the clouds to the lowlands or leach through the soils into mountain streams that feed the rivers that interlace the country?

Mount Mitchell and the other high altitude peaks of this area have given us warning of the danger to life that airborne pollution presents. By studying the information that research reveals and eventually making the hard choices necessary to prevent pollution, we may be able to reverse the damage done to these ancient mountains.

In saving the forests, we may be saving ourselves.

Russell Putman, Buladean fiddle player

BULADEAN DANCE

BULADEAN, N. C.—Saturday nights are usually quiet here in this small community on the Tennessee border. A few tires screeching and maybe a disturbed rooster crowing break the silence. But one weekend things were different.

The Russell Putman String Band assembled at the Buladean Firehall to play and folks came arunning. It's not often there's a community dance here, or music either, so those who like to flatfoot it, or just tap their toes flocked in.

Jess Sheets, who has bussed several generations of area students to the elementary school, gazed approvingly at the crowd.

"It's a good thing to get people together. I'm glad to see it," he said.

When Russell Putman on the fiddle, Will Ruggles on the guitar, and Bob Carlin on the banjo broke into the first song, the crowd, seated and standing around the edges of the fire hall, tapped and swayed but were reluctant to start the dancing. Some folks here still frown on such doings as the devil's work.

But when an innocent three-year-old found himself moved by the music to step out and cavort in a freestyle jig to the seductive rhythm, others gradually found their way onto the floor.

Old-time flatfooting started off the evening; but after a few numbers, Frank Jenkins from nearby Penland volunteered to call some dances. He organized and instructed, then put people through their paces.

Some of the folks maintained their traditional mountain independence and improvised their own variations, but everyone had a good time.

Such traditional tunes as "Little Maggie" and "Little Log Cabin in the Lane" reminded people of their roots and reinforced the sense of pride in the local talent who played for their neighbors.

Buladean Firehall was a good place to be Saturday night.

Even the little ones enjoyed the music.

Frank Jenkins led the crowd in a square dance.

A HOUSE WITH TWO SMOKES

BULADEAN, N.C.—Most of us don't think much about tradition and "the old ways" except during the holidays. Then we put up a tree, cook a big meal and exchange gifts, or on New Year's Day we cook black-eyed peas with a penny for good luck. But on January second we leave tradition behind and carry on with our contemporary lifestyles.

However, in the rural parts of the Appalachian Mountains, people continue traditions in their daily lives.

As you're taking a drive through the country, especially during the cooler seasons, you may notice two smoke streams rising from many of the older houses. The smoke from the large, central chimney signals a heating fire, while the smoke rising from the smaller chimney at the back of the house means just one thing—good cooking.

Mary Burleson, a Mitchell County, North Carolina, native, lives in one of those houses with "two smokes." She is carrying on the tradition of wood stove cooking, not as nostalgic homage, but as part of her life.

"Why up 'til 40 years ago every house in these parts had two smokes. We didn't have electricity so we did all our cooking on a wood stove back then," Mrs. Burleson remembered.

Today Mrs. Burleson's kitchen has all of the electrical conveniences of any modern kitchen: a range, oven, coffee maker, water heater, and even a microwave oven. But standing in one corner is the main attraction of her kitchen—a large, old Home Comfort wood cook stove.

This Home Comfort isn't just for decoration, either.

"I still use it a whole lot in the winter," she explained. "In the summertime I don't hardly use it 'cause it makes the whole house too hot. But on cold days I'll use it for most everything, except baking cakes. You need steady heat to make cakes that don't fall and you don't always get that with the old stoves."

The day I visited Mrs. Burleson's house, it was quite cold outside but the kitchen was hot—very hot.

She was canning sausage and ribs from the hogs her husband, Howard, had slaughtered in late November. Already she had "put up" 20 cans and was working on the last batch while we chatted.

Mrs. Burleson explained that she has been using a pressure cooker for only the past seven or eight years. "Before that I had to do all my canning in a big open pot. I had to put a sheet in the bottom and cloths between the jars to keep them from breaking.

"You think it's hot now? We had to cook each run for four hours at a time back then. The pressure cooker takes less than half that long."

As she wiped her brow she said, "I always do my canning on the old stove. It gets warm in here, but it's worth it because it saves me on my electric bill."

Up until 1984, Mrs. Burleson saved even more on her electric bill.

"Besides heating water in the reservoir on the side here," she said, while gesturing to the well on the right side of her stove, "We had a regular water heater hooked up to the back of the stove. See those two holes? Well, pipes used to run through there and we'd heat all of our bath and dishes water with the fire. And it got hotter than the electric heater gets it, too."

When the old heater tank rusted out, Mrs. Burleson replaced it with a more convenient electric one.

"I decided to get the electric one so I wouldn't have to keep my fire going all of the time," she said.

In the days when most fires were going all of the time, cooks often used the stoves like today's crock pot. Anything that needed a long, slow cooking was just set on the back of the stove and allowed to simmer all day.

This method turned out delicious soups and incredible beans—soup beans, as Mrs. Burleson calls them.

"There's nothing my boys liked better, when they was home, than good soup beans," she said proudly.

"Well, to make soup beans," she began—somewhat incredulous that anyone might not already know—"you start with dried beans, October beans or birdseye will do. Parboil them for thirty minutes, then wash them in cold water, put a piece of fat pork in, cover them with fresh water and cook 'em 'til the soup gets thick on 'em. You'll have to keep pouring the water to them 'til they get thick."

Cooking beans this way on an electric range would be impractical because of the expense of the electricity, but on the wood stove the method is just perfect.

"Howard fills a room in the garage with good dried wood. That'll last me for two years."

Mrs. Burleson serves soup beans "as a meal in itself" some days, but not on Sunday.

"Usually on Sunday my boys come and bring their families for dinner. Then we'll have soup beans or my own canned green beans as a side dish."

Each Sunday morning Mrs. Burleson gets up early to start her fire so that she and Howard can have a big breakfast and to build a bed of coals that will last all morning. Demonstrating how she starts her fire "in a hurry," Mrs. Burleson grabbed a metal dust pan and a small shovel, part of a fireplace set.

"Howard's fire has burned down lots of good red coals by morning," she explained as she opened the front of the Fisher stove which heats the home.

"So I get a big scoop of his fire and carry it into the kitchen and throw it into my firebox and put some good dry wood in on top of it. Usually it goes right up.

"Now just keep wood in the stove all the time. Don't ever let it burn out if you want to keep the temperature up. Just as quick as it burns down a little, fill it back up and after a while she'll go to cooking."

Once the fire gets going, Mary fixes fresh biscuits with brown gravy, fried tenderloins and "home grown eggs."

"You just can't beat country eggs. We raise over forty hens just so's we'll have fresh eggs," she said. "After breakfast I'll cook my dinner partly, before we go to church, so's I won't have so much to do when the children are here," she said. "The children" include her four sons, three daughters-in-law, and several of her grandchildren.

When the family returns from church, the house is always toasty warm and filled with good smells coming from Mrs. Burleson's kitchen where food has been simmering for two or three hours. Her fire will usually "keep" through Sunday school and church but needs immediate attention when the family walks in so that the oven will be hot enough for making bread.

A typical Sunday dinner will include beans, Irish potatoes, biscuits and corn bread, sweet potatoes—"I either boil them or cut them in half and put butter and a little brown sugar on them"—and fried chicken or chicken and dumplings.

"Now, some have trouble making good dumplings," Mrs. Burleson said, "but I think they're easy. You just take the broth off a chicken. Pour it into a pan with enough milk to do you, and a half stick of butter.

"Bring it to a boil. Then you make your biscuit dough. To make dumplings, I roll them and pat them in my hand—real thin—but some roll them out with a pin and cut them. Anyway you do it, just drop the biscuits down in the boiling pan and cook them 'til they're done."

Mrs. Burleson wasn't trying to be vague in order to keep secret family recipes, she has just made biscuits and dumplings for so long that she really doesn't use measurements.

"That's the way my mommy always done," she explained. "Now, I've got measuring cups and spoons and recipes but I don't use them. I've just got it in my head and I use enough to make it taste the way I like it."

But why, in this day of automation, and with the more convenient appliances available, would anyone choose to go to all the trouble of cooking on a wood stove?

"Well, it doesn't seem like that much trouble to me," Mrs. Burleson said matter-of-factly.

However, it might seem like a lot of trouble to the modern chef since the fire box has to be loaded every hour or so to maintain a high, or steady, temperature. Also, since the temperature rises and falls as the fire is stoked and burns down, the food needs to be carefully watched, often stirred.

Cooking with fire is a mess, too. The ash tin has to be emptied regularly, and occasionally soot must be removed from the interior of the stove.

"Cleaning the soot out is only a little worse than cleaning the kitchen afterwards," Mrs. Burleson quipped. "When I clean it I take out about a bushel at a time. Then I have to sweep and dust and mop the whole room."

So, again, why would anyone go to all this trouble when the electric range stands idly by?

Part of it is tradition or heritage. "It's just the way I've always done it," Mrs. Burleson said, but the other reason is the final product that comes out of the old stoves.

Mrs. Burleson explained: "You've heard people say, 'Food just doesn't taste like my grandma's used to?' Well, sir, it wasn't the recipes she used or even the cook's touch. It was the old cook stove she used for so many years. It was seasoned."

Just as corn bread is better out of an old, blackened, cast-iron skillet because of all of the good food that's been in the pan, the old stoves absorb the flavors of years of fine cooking and enhance the flavor of the dish.

The design of the stove also adds to the quality of finished wood stove meals. Rather than the coiled heat that is produced by electric ranges, the wood stove plates are heated evenly with the temperature distributed from "high"—the plate directly over the firebox—to medium and low as the plates are further and further to the right, away from the heat source.

And instead of the heating elements above and below the food as in an electric oven, a good cook stove surrounds the food with heat, cooking it from all sides. The stoves are designed to draw the heat through the double walls around the entire oven cavity.

This design provides perfect conditions for making breads, both baking powder breads and yeast breads. They end up with a light crust on all sides, cooked evenly through.

It is hard to say whether Mrs. Burleson's biscuits or corn bread is better. Recipes vary, of course, but Mrs. Burleson likes her corn bread without an egg.

"I always clabber a little bit of my milk to make sour milk—buttermilk, some calls it. That sour milk is self-rising and so you don't need the egg," she said.

But beware, Mrs. Burleson's milk most likely isn't like yours.

Indeed, as a result of another tradition Mrs. Burleson continues, she has some of the best milk available. All her life she has tried to keep a couple of cows so that she will have fresh milk. Twice a day she goes to the barn and milks the cows herself.

"Why, it's a lot more expensive keeping these cows than it would be if I bought milk at the store," she said over her shoulder while tugging on a cow's teat, filling her bucket with white, foaming milk. "Even with what I make selling a little to my neighbors, I'd still be better off buying it. But I love to have them, I've always had them. Besides, you can't make good sour milk with store milk." However, you can make it with Mrs. Burleson's milk.

For $1.50 you can get a gallon of milk from her. Let it rest for a day in the refrigerator, and a good two inches of cream will rise to the top.

"Now the store milk just don't have that kind of cream in it," she said with a smile.

If you've ever tasted fresh—really fresh—milk and eggs or good wood stove cooked food, you'll understand why someone like Mary Burleson goes to all the trouble to carry on old traditions.

Mary and Howard Burleson testing the day's apple butter.

The living room still has Sandburg's guitar and other personal effects.

THE CARL SANDBURG HOME

FLAT ROCK, N.C.—Carl Sandburg believed in the paradoxes of life. He once wrote, "Truth consists of paradoxes and a paradox is two facts that stand on opposite hillsides and across the intervening valley call each other names."

Located in Flat Rock, which for more than a century served as a retreat for the aristocrats of Charleston, South Carolina, is Connemara, a 240-acre estate first owned by Christopher Memminger, secretary of the Confederate Treasury. In 1945 the people's poet, the former Socialist Sandburg, who wrote the six-volume biography of Abraham Lincoln, moved with his family to the estate where he spent his last 22 years.

After Sandburg's death in 1967 at 89, the United States Department of the Interior bought Connemara. In 1968 Congress established the Carl Sandburg Home National Historic Site, which is administered by the National Park Service and is open to the public daily except for Thanksgiving, Christmas, and New Year's Day.

A visit to the Carl Sandburg Home takes you into his life and gives insight into his values. Sandburg himself hides among the books that line the walls and flits ahead of you from room to room, each one filled with his presence.

Once Sandburg listed his requirements for a happy life. He said, "1. To be out of jail. 2. To eat and sleep regular. 3. To get what I write printed in a free country for free people. 4. To have a little love at home and a little affection and esteem outside the home."

How these requirements formed his life becomes clear as you walk through Connemara. Sitting on a hillside which commands an open view of the far mountains, you see the house is certainly no jail, and the extensive trails that thread through the estate show a wandering spirit.

On the main floor of the house is the dining room, which also served as the Sandburgs' family room. The poet's place is set as in life, his red-capped thermos sitting beside his plate with its promise of hot, fresh coffee. Echoes of the clash of cutlery competing with Sandburg's deep voice drift just beyond the ear.

Sleep came to the poet on the top floor in a small bedroom next to his crowded office where he worked from late evening to early morning before retiring. He awoke from mid-to-late-morning to listen to music in his bedroom while he exercised lightly.

Evidence of his writing success is everywhere, as is the response to his work. Books, newspaper and magazine clippings, reviews, and articles fill shelves, lie on tables and rest on chairs, just as they did during Sandburg's occupancy.

The love of his family speaks from Mrs. Sandburg's warm office where she managed her world-famous goat operation and kept the household accounts, freeing her husband to devote his energies to writing. His children's and grandchildren's bedrooms also tell of the family affection that surrounded him at Connemara.

The simple joys that filled Sandburg's life continue to fill his home. Small bowls holding leaves, nuts, buckeyes, and colorful stones speak of his habit of bringing bits of the outdoors into his house. Collages of newspaper and magazine illustrations repeat his fascination with art and life.

And shelves and shelves of books shout volumes about his love for the printed word. As a poet, newspaperman, essayist, novelist, and historian, he read and wrote with a gargantuan appetite.

The grounds of the estate tell of his love of nature, the well-trod trails showing his rambling propensities.

The goat barn with its flock of curious, gregarious goats maintains a living link with the Sandburgs. Mrs. Sandburg's wish to expand her goat herd brought the family to North Carolina. While his wife ran the goat enterprise, the poet enjoyed the antics of the boisterous goats and was proud of his wife's success as a breeder and dairy operator.

In addition to the estate's silent recounting of Sandburg's life and habits, knowledgeable tour guides and a videotape provide an excellent introduction to the world of Carl Sandburg.

Bess Gibbs, one of the guides, peoples the empty rooms with anecdotes and descriptions of the Sandburg family and their life at Connemara. Her affection for the poet and her respect for his way of life bring the estate to life.

The videotape, based on an Edward R. Murrow broadcast, provides visitors with a chance to see and hear the poet read his work, sing his songs, and explain his philosophy of life. One quotation in particular helps explain his nearly universal appeal.

When asked what was the most detestable word in the English language, Sandburg replied, "exclusiveness."

He then explained, "When you are exclusive you shut out a more or less large range of humanity from your mind and heart—from your understanding of them."

There is no pretension or aristocratic "exclusiveness" evident at the Sandburg estate. The wooden crates Sandburg used still hold his papers and support his old typewriter. Piles of books and mounds of paper still show the author's preoccupations. That the family lived in the house with comfort rather than kept it as a showplace is clear on each floor.

Reading his poems will open Sandburg's mind to you, but a visit to

These goats were direct descendants of those owned by Mrs. Sandburg.

Sandburg's Office

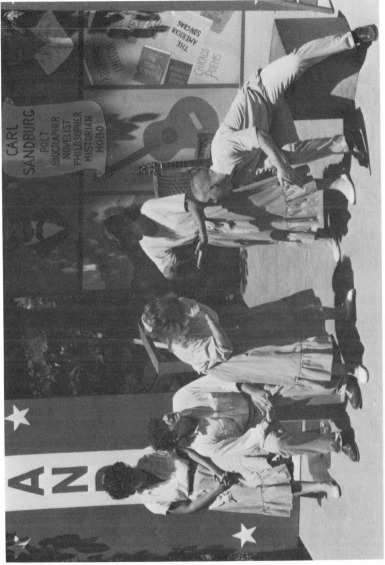

Interns from the Flat Rock Playhouse perform a skit about Sandburg's life and work.

his home shows you his life. While his works of art are important, the man himself surpasses his collected poems, his novel, and his biography of Lincoln.

A day at Connemara will introduce you to the larger work of art, Carl Sandburg.

VANCE BIRTHPLACE

REEMS CREEK, N.C. — "The history of the world is but the biography of great men," wrote Thomas Carlyle, English historian and philosopher. The history of North Carolina is no different.

Zebulon Baird Vance, born in Reems Creek Valley in 1830, came down from the mountains to guide North Carolina during the turmoil of the Civil War and remained in politics for the rest of his life to help the state recover after the defeat of the Confederacy. To honor his name and to educate his people, the state has created a unique exhibit.

The Vance Birthplace, located about 12 miles north of Asheville, is a State Historic Site featuring reconstructed hand-hewn log buildings. The two-story log house which is the birthplace, a tool house, a loom house, a smoke house, a slave house, a spring house, and a corn crib re-create the farm as it was in Vance's youth. A modern visitors center at the site houses museum exhibits, an information center, a theatre where a slide show presents Vance's life, and the administrative offices.

"We're here because this was his birthplace, but also because the reconstruction represents the lifestyles of the 1830s common to the people of Western North Carolina. We also serve as the place that tells the history of Vance's career; we're a memorial to his career," says David Tate, site director.

Educated at Washington College Academy near Jonesborough, Tennessee, at Newton Academy in Asheville, and at the University of North Carolina in Chapel Hill, Vance practiced law, served in the North Carolina House, was the colonel of a Confederate regiment, then the governor of North Carolina for three terms before entering the United States House of Representatives. His life ended during his fourth term as a United States senator.

"Perhaps more than any other individual, Zebulon Baird Vance typified the strength and sturdy virtues, as well as the independence and intellectual capacities of the people making the mountains of Western North Carolina their home," wrote Ora Blackmun in her **Western North Carolina: Its Mountains and its People to 1880**.

A visit to his birthplace clearly shows the truth of this high praise. The 15-minute slide show that covers Vance's childhood, education, and his legal, military and political careers is an excellent introduction to the man and his times. It shows his importance to not only the history of his native state, but to that of the South and the country as a whole.

The restored house is constructed around the original chimney which has stood since 1795. Filling the sitting room, three bedrooms and

Grounds of the Vance Birthplace. Main house is on the right.

View from an upstairs window of the main house.

Spinning and weaving house

kitchen are furnishings of the first half of the 19th century. For example, the quilts:

"This is an actual quilt made in the early 1800s," says Tate, pointing to a blue, patterned beauty in an upstairs bedroom. "Everything in the house dates back to the 1800s and is fairly similar to what the Vances would have had. And we do have some of the actual pieces that the Vances owned."

The large spinning wheel and a yarn winder in the loom house are Vance family pieces that have survived the years to find a home back where they first served well over a century ago.

Twice a year the Vance home comes alive for Pioneer Living Days, when costumed staff members and volunteers demonstrate the skills and practices of the early settlers.

"In the spring, the third Sunday in April, we have demonstrations of the domestic skills typical of the 1830s," Tate said. "And in the third weekend in September we have a two-day demonstration which includes a reenacted militia event."

On these days the huge old fireplaces are put to work, and cooking, churning butter, weaving and other crafts fill the house and outbuildings with activity that would make Zeb Vance feel right at home.

From November 1 through March 31, the Vance Birthplace is open Tuesday through Saturday from 10 a.m. to 4 p.m. and Sunday from 1-4 p.m. and is closed on Monday. During the other seasons, the hours are 9-5 Monday through Saturday and 12-5 Sunday.

The Zebulon B. Vance Birthplace can be reached from the Blue Ridge Parkway by following signs from milepost 375.5, and it can be reached from highway 19-23 by following the signs just south of Weaverville.

The history of the mountains becomes a palpable lesson at the Vance Birthplace.

Warren Campbell with hand-made harness.

HARNESS MAKER

BULADEAN, N.C.—Horses and harnesses are parts of a bygone age to most Americans, replaced by horsepower and seat belts.

But in the mountains of Western North Carolina and East Tennessee, Belgians and other work horses continue to wear heavy harnesses to pull heavier loads or to plow the rich soil worn from the millenia-old heights.

Warren Campbell of Buladean is one man who ensures this equine tradition will endure for a few more years. His harness-filled barn supplies horse masters for miles around, and he's been known to do a bit of horse-trading on the side.

"Every once in awhile I'll trade a horse," he says with an ironic smile. "I traded a horse or two long about since I was 14 year old."

Campbell will be 67 in October, so a few horses (work horses) have passed through his expert hands.

"I don't hardly trade on riding horses, and I don't trade on no broken down ones," he says. "I like a good built horse with a pretty head, carries itself good, upright."

He has learned about horses since his childhood, a time when every farm had two or three horses to work. But even in the mountains, time has brought change.

"Most people just got too lazy to work horses. I did, I am. You see all this mountain land growing up since people got rid of their horses. You can't work a tractor on a steep hill," he says, sweeping his hand towards the tops of the steep ridge running up behind his barn.

However, for those hardy, hard-working farmers who have stuck with their horses, Warren Campbell can supply the needed tack. Some harness he buys new and resells; some he buys old, disassembles, rearranges, and reassembles; some he makes from scratch.

"I like to help my friends and sell stuff. I peck around and can sell for a whole lot less than if they go out to buy 'em. It's a little job, but it keeps a feller from loafering."

Campbell starts with a half a horse hide.

"Genuine harness leather is what it is; cowhide is sort of thin for harness," he says. "I go pick it up in Fredericksburg, Ohio. Saves shipping—it's so bulky and hard to handle.

"It's all done with hand tools, about. I ain't got no fancy equipment. I ain't in no hurry."

His tools and materials have accumulated over the years. Much of his leather working equipment he has bought used.

"I bought out a leather worker out of Elizabethton toward Watauga, Tennessee. I got a lot of his stuff that I needed," he says, displaying some of his leather stamps.

In a similar way he gets his materials.

"Like hames, brass knob hames. I still go around the country and buy 'em off people, wherever I can hear of someone who has some to sell. I buy off first one, then another.

"A lot of these hames is 60-75 year old, I know," he says. "But you can't hardly get any anymore."

The winter months with their frozen fields and snowy pastures are good for harness work. The planting, tending, and harvesting are past and ahead, and it's time for loading the hooks in his barn with harness and chains, bridles and halters.

Assisting Campbell with his work is his 4-year-old grandson, Travis Parker. Skills and interests that have flowed down to Warren Campbell from his Scottish ancestors who first arrived in the high mountains are being absorbed by the youngest generation.

"I had a horse that used to follow Travis around everywhere. He'd set his chin on Travis' head and walk with him," recalls Campbell.

Even when Travis climbs aboard his four-wheel, all-terrain vehicle, dangling behind are several sets of horse lead chains, visible links to the past forming a clear mountain symbol.

To see Warren Campbell's wares, drive across Iron Mountain Gap into Buladean, turn up Blevins Branch Road, and look for the wagon wheels on either side of his driveway; he's used to visitors.

"I sell right here. Some comes from off; some from right around. Just here and yonder," says Campbell.

Or you can look for him and his harness in Kingsport.

"I sell some over at the Kingsport Livestock Market. I go over every two weeks or a month," he says.

Whether you are looking for a horse or a harness, or simply in need of some home style wisdom, Warren Campbell's your man. He's seen the flow and ebb of the work horse, and he still says with confidence, "I think a lot of folks will go back to 'em; a horse can do things a tractor just can't."

CULLIFER FAMILY

BULADEAN, N.C.—Self-reliance, independence, love and respect for the land, hard work—these were the watchwords for the rugged pioneers who settled the Southern Appalachians more than two centuries ago.

Today these words echo for a new kind of pioneer trying to establish his family in these mountains. John Cullifer, a success in the business world, has left that life behind to begin to forge a new life—one full of independence, self-reliance, caring for the land, and of course, hard work.

Not your typical Florida transplant, Cullifer lives in the mountains on the mountains' terms. Not interested in squeezing money from the land but in cooperating with it to live a simple but full life, he has brought his family here to experience a natural existence.

"All our problems get back to man messing up nature," Cullifer explains. "We intend to farm completely organically, to become self-sufficient on our own land, raising food without chemicals, poisons, and antibiotics. Taking care of the land so it will take care of us."

His land (38 acres) rises from a clear-running trout stream up to steep, wooded ridges, a typical mountain cove that has been farmed off and on for over a century.

"We took two 7,000 mile trips to find our farm," he recalls, smiling. "We looked all over this country and into Canada. But once we had seen this area, we just couldn't stay away from here."

Walking across his land, Cullifer points out his projects with pride—a large log house under construction, the gardens, a trout pond, the old hog pen, then the new pen built from his own logs, his horse corral, his rabbit hutch and quail pens, his flock of guinea hens, his peacock and peahen, and most importantly, his goat barn and goats, the mainstay of his farm.

"We're doing everything exactly how we want it," he says.

The log cabin he is building is already an impressive structure. Raised by hand using poplar logs cut on the steep woodlands above, the skeletal house stands ready for completion.

"Eventually we will fill it with all handmade furniture," he says.

When asked how he knows how to build a house from the ground up, using materials found on his own property, Cullifer smiles before answering, "Whatever I get interested in, I get a book and learn about it. I believe in self-education, probably because I've had to educate myself throughout my life."

The small building that houses the Cullifers while their log house is constructed bursts at the seams with books and magazines that have taught him.

"I like to keep up with things. We get the newspaper, 25-30 magazines regularly, and I watch the news on television. Even though I'm living on my mountain, I stay in touch with the world," he explains, as he pulls the book on building log cabins from a stuffed bookcase.

Books have also told him how to farm organically to escape the dangers of living in a society that uses chemicals and posions and antibiotics as a shortcut to large harvests.

Cultivating his farm without herbicides and pesticides has not been easy, Cullifer admits. Thick weeds choked most of the area when he bought the farm; however, when advised by experts to use herbicides, he refused.

"I don't care what anyone says," Cullifer emphatically says. "If you keep digging them up and chopping them down, eventually you can control the weeds. That field above the house was thick with weeds, blackberry vines, goldenrod, etc. Already I have it under control through work, not poisons.

"One reason for keeping all my guinea hens," he says, gesturing towards the flock of grey fowl busily scratching about, "is to control garden pests. In the summer from daylight to dark they troop up one row of the garden, then down the next eating insects."

When asked about controlling groundhogs and rabbits, he laughs, "From one organic gardening book I learned not to kill them, but to feed them. I plant three or four rows of cheap beans on the edges of the garden and let them eat that. So far they haven't gone into the center where my crops are."

His love of wildlife becomes apparent as Cullifer explains his plans for raising different varieties of grasses to attract wild animals to that upper part of his land.

Cooperating with nature, not fighting her, is his intention. The fertility of the mountains, if properly husbanded, can sustain both man and beasts, he believes.

"You can control pests and diseases through biological and organic means," Cullifer explains. "I'm amazed at how well things grow in these mountains simply through hard work and lending nature a hand. We have three freezers full of our own meat, and produce, and 40 cases of our canned goods stored away.

"I had to sell a hog this week because I had no place to put the meat if we had slaughtered it," he says. "Our hogs do real well because

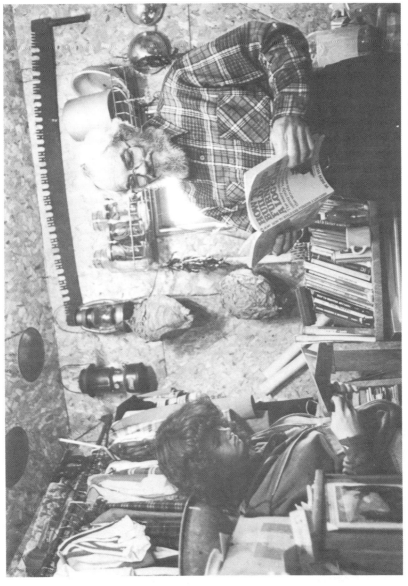

John Cullifer looks through a book on building log cabins while his daughter, Sandi, also reads.

we feed them hog pellets mixed with goat milk. Right now we don't have a market for the milk, so we use it that way."

Despite the lack of a milk market, goats are Cullifer's money crop. He raises the does for sale as dairy goats.

"The hardest thing about raising goats is having to sell the ones you've raised from newborn kids," he says. "I know each goat individually. If I'm up in the woods and hear one holler down here, I know just who it is."

Cullifer's goats are La Manchas, a breed that originated in the United States. Coming in a variety of colors, these friendly creatures with strange ears make a visit to their barnyard a game. Any stray flap or piece of paper is nibbled. They demand to be noticed and petted.

"They have the best disposition of any breed," Cullifer says proudly. "There's a lot of La Mancha breeding in the mountains, a danger of inbreeding, so I'm hoping to find a buck out west to bring in a new bloodline."

The does are bred in August to freshen (deliver) in January, the slack time of year for the Cullifers. They bring the small kids into their house for warmth if necessary.

Although this past year's crop of kids didn't fulfill expectations— only one doe out of 10 kids—Cullifer expects things to even out in the long run. This year's does are about to freshen, and eventually he plans to keep 15 does to deliver two or three kids apiece.

"Goats do well here because they were originally mountain creatures," he explains. "By nature they are comfortable from 15 degrees to 85 degrees."

Once the does freshen and the kids are weaned, milking becomes a family enterprise. "When we're milking we're on a schedule. Every 12 hours they must be milked," Cullifer says, as he fills a stainless steel bucket with foaming milk from one of his does who lost three kids this past week in a premature delivery.

While he milks, Sandi and Johnnie, his two youngest daughters, give vitamins to the rest of the goats, then feed them. There is plenty of work for all on the Cullifer farm.

The Cullifers are in the third year of a five-year plan for accomplishing the transition from the city to the farming life. For now, Mrs. Cullifer spends her winters in Florida overseeing the family's business interests, but soon the whole family will be established in their land.

Everyone must work to bring the dream to reality, but there seems little worry about that. From Fred the horse to Silver Heels the buck goat, everyone does his best to create an independent, self-reliant family farm.

The ideals of the eighteenth century still direct the lives of these twentieth century pioneers.

One view from Mount Mitchell looks down the Black Mountains with Roan Mountain in the distance.

HIGHEST HOME IN THE EAST

MOUNT MITCHELL, N.C.—Living on the highest mountain in the East has its advantages and disadvantages, especially in the winter. Just ask John Sharpe, superintendent of Mount Mitchell State Park.

Whether the weather is clear and sunny or snow whips by in zero degree temperatures and hurricane force winds, Sharpe, his wife Ginger, and their small dog Buford are at home in their house on the crest of the Black Mountains, where this year dense clouds and cold rain predominate so far.

"I came to Mount Mitchell hoping I'd see a lot of snow and cold weather in the winter. This is my third winter and so far they've been mild," said Sharpe recently on a day with thick clouds and horizontally blown rain keeping visibility on the mountain at zero.

The average snowfall in the park is 104 inches a year, but according to Sharpe the past two years have provided less than half that amount.

"Last year we had only 43 inches," he said with some disappointment.

Ginger, Sharpe's wife of a year, also wants to see more snow.

"I got cross country skis for Christmas, and I want to use them," she said.

One positive aspect of the warmer weather has been the effect on the mountain wildlife, although this too is not an unqualified benefit.

"The mild winters have allowed more animals to survive. The mammal population is exceptional, way above normal," said Sharpe.

Red squirrels, rabbits, rats, mice, voles, and deer have thriven.

"Out our living room window we see deer grazing. Buford loves that," said Sharpe.

"Buford just loves to look at the deer. It's a ritual; everyday we take him for a drive to see the deer," said Ginger.

However, along with the increase of cute, furry mammals has come a growth in the bear and wildcat populations. The bears especially have caused some problems.

"We've got claw marks all over the side of our house. Sometimes when I cook, they smell the food and come up to see what's for supper," said Ginger.

"One day I heard a noise. I opened the shades, and there I was, face-to-face with a bear," she said.

Keeping a sense of humor is important when dealing with park bears. Sharpe's laughter showed that he's adapted to large mammal problems.

"We've had more problems with bears than we'd had for several years up here. This summer they started raiding garbage cans, cars and scaring campers. I had to warn anyone who was going to camp in the campground that a bear would be through in the night and to put everything up carefully.

"If there's a trash can or garbage available, they'll get into it. Once when we brought in a load of groceries, I heard a noise and looked up to see a bear rummaging through the dump truck. At the same time he looked at us, sniffed, then went back to his rummaging," said Sharpe.

Obtaining those groceries is one aspect of life on the mountain that took some getting used to for Sharpe and his wife. There is no super-market around the corner. Even as the raven flies it would take a while to get a loaf of bread, and the ravens don't deliver.

"We have to drive 35 miles to get to the nearest grocery store. Even the closest little store is 22 miles one way. If we want a loaf of bread or jug of milk we have to drive 44 miles," said Sharpe.

"Yes, that's one of the hardest things is keeping up on the groceries. It takes a lot of planning," said Ginger.

While it's a long way to the store, there is no real isolation from people most of the year. Although attendance drops dramatically once the fall color season passes, as long as the Blue Ridge Parkway is open, people drop by throughout the winter.

"Visitation slows down a whole lot. It depends on the weather. We may drop to only 300 a month, but if the weather is good we can get 3,000 or so in the winter.

"In fact, our attendance increases with the snow. A day or two after a snowfall the roads are clear—we plow down to highway 80—and people will drive up to see the snow. We get calls from Florida, Georgia, all over the Southeast from people who want to know if we have any snow to come up to see," said Sharpe.

With the reduced numbers of visitors comes a chance for Sharpe and his staff to work on maintenance that can't be done with the summer and fall crowds around. Although all his seasonal employees are gone, he still has a ranger and two maintenance mechanics to work with.

"This is the time of year we can get a lot done repairing facilities, fixing trails, and doing inside work. Summertimes are spent just keeping up with breakdowns," said Sharpe.

However, he also loses his clerk-typist, who is a summer employee.

"Well, I enjoy the fact that we don't have as much visitation, but so much of my job is administrative that I spend more time in the office than I do in the summer. I end up doing all of the secretarial work myself," Sharpe said with a grimace.

Nonetheless, for this superintendent, one advantage outweighs all of the problems of his job—the beauty of his park and the views from it.

Sharpe stands beside Elisha Mitchell's grave.

"It's a beautiful place to live. Sometimes we're at eye level with the clouds. Yesterday we could look to the east—everything below Table Rock was in the clouds, the mountaintops sticking up. They looked like islands out in the ocean.

"I'll probably stay here until I retire," said Sharpe.

Sharpe opens park gate.

APPALACHIAN TRAIL

There are two Appalachian Trails—the physical 2,100 mile path that runs along the high mountain ridges of 14 eastern states, and the **Trail**, an idea carried throughout the world by those who have hiked its demanding miles.

Stretching from Springer Mountain, Georgia, to Mount Katahdin, Maine, the Appalachian Trail is one of the longest marked footpaths in the world. Each spring many hikers set out to make the long journey. Many fail, but others succeed. Well over a thousand hikers have made the end-to-end trek, an accomplishment each carries with pride.

But for every one of this elite group, thousands more have hiked some portion of the trail, whether on day outings, overnight hikes, or trips of hundreds of miles.

No cheering crowds, fat professional contracts, or commercial endorsements are found along the trail or at its end. Hiking is not a sport that provides a chance to prove oneself better than others, and hikers don't defeat the mountains they climb or the valleys they cross.

Peace and serenity travel the trail, together with hard work and sore muscles.

Whether traveling through fields of early spring flowers, or enclosed in the green world of the summer corridor through the trees, or walking across the open summit of a majestic bald enjoying the far-stretching beauty of blazing fall colors, or crunching through snow on a winter's day, the hiker's success or failure rests on him alone and his values.

Benton MacKaye, the father of the Appalachian Trail who in 1921 first proposed its creation, explained the wonder of the trail, "With pollution and overpopulation spawning a sprawling urban desert, I am encouraged by the knowledge that there are millions in America who care about wilderness and mountains; who go forth for strength to Mother Earth; who defend her domain and seek her secrets. I am proud to have played a role in the birth of the Appalachian Trail. And I am proud of the generations of hikers who have made my dream a reality."

The late Julian M. Maddox was one of these hikers. He hiked the whole trail, he served as president of the Carolina Hiking Club, and he kept on the **Trail** until the time he died. His final request was that his body be cremated and his ashes scattered in the mountains.

"Since he loved the Appalachian Trail so much, we thought that should be the place," recalls his daughter-in-law, Dr. Jeanette Maddox, a Burnsville, North Carolina, veterinarian.

His family drove to Carver's Gap at Roan Mountain where the

Appalachian Trail runs. They honored his passing by walking the bald summits he loved and leaving his ashes to enrich them. His spirit will ever be on the **Trail**.

This long narrow ribbon along the mountain crests of the East captures people in different ways.

"In 1977 I took a non-credit course at the University of Tennessee in backpacking," remembers Jana McGrane, while walking through the snow with her husband Jim on a warm February day. "We went on four weekend backpacking trips, mostly in the Smokies. I've been coming back to the trail ever since."

When asked what season she found most enjoyable on the AT, as veterans refer to it, she hesitated before answering, "That's hard . . . I especially enjoy June because of the rhododendron blossoms and the flame azaleas. The flowers are my favorites. Lots to identify: flowering trees, flowering bushes, flowering fields. At times the whole trail looks like it's decorated for a wedding."

But on this first day of February, snow fills the trail, snow stretches away on all sides beneath the trees, and snow makes the going wet and slow.

"Being the first person to walk over the virgin snow of the trail, seeing the small animal tracks running from tree to tree, listening to the quiet— these all make it worthwhile today," she said.

Her husband agreed.

"What I enjoy most at this time of year is being able to see clearly how the land lies," Jim said. "In the summer, leaves and the haze make it difficult to see the landscapes you're walking though most of the time. Also, I enjoy the challenge. You have to push yourself harder in the winter to get through the snow, especially on the uphill sections."

Their trek along the top of Iron Mountain to Little Rock Knob provides plenty of "uphill sections." The last leg of the hike climbs steeply through a rhododendron tunnel, up slippery rocks, to reach the pinnacle, where a rocky perch above a vertical rock face provides a stirring view of Tennessee to the north and North Carolina to the south.

"A view like this rewards a lot of hard work," said Jim as he dried his socks, or at least attempted to, sitting in the sun above the precipitous drop-off. "I'll carry this hike with me for a long time."

Surveying the valley before her and the mountains stretching around her to the horizon, Jan silently nodded agreement as she gathered strength for the trip back down the trail to Greasy Creek Gap.

Many reasons urge people to the Appalachian Trail. Personal disaster sent Dan Everett. He came through this stretch in mid-October on his way from Georgia to Maine, where he started in early April. A serious automobile accident, a split with his fiancée, and general confusion took him from Ohio to the Appalachian Trail, although he had never hiked before to any extent.

"I didn't know what to do with myself. I had a good job with General Motors as a designer, but I felt empty. Somehow the idea of walking the trail came to me," he recalled as he rested under an overhanging rock that overlooks the Limestone Cove area.

"After two days on the trail in Maine, I was ready to quit, but by the time I reached a place where I could get off, I was much stronger and enjoying myself, so here I am.

"I learned a lot on the trail," Dan said, "things I can't put into words but that have made me a different person than I was before. You could say that I was born again during my hike. I learned to trust and have faith."

Some of the most beautiful parts of the entire trail make up the northern rim of the Toe River Valley in places: the magical balds of the Roan massif. the ancient trail along Iron Mountain, the winding climb up to Unaka, the spectacular view at Beauty Spot, and the descent down to the Nolichucky, the river that the Toe turns into after plunging through the Nolichucky gorge, then up to Little and Big Bald.

Access to the trail is easy, since in many places it runs along the Tennessee-North Carolina line and this crosses some major highways. Indian Grave Gap, Iron Mountain Gap, Hughes Gap, and Carver's Gap are just a few of the places at which the trail intersects public roads.

For more information about the Appalachian Trail in North Carolina or in its entirety, write the Appalchian Trail Conference, P.O. Box 807, Harper's Ferry, West Virginia 25425-0807.

Enjoy your trail. Founder Benton MacKaye's words simply state its "ultimate purpose . . . to walk, to see, to see what you see." In today's confusion, such simplicity is its own reward.

View from Little Rock Knob on the Appalachian Trail.

Kevin Hollifield slips his feet into a crack on Harpoon.

ROCK CLIMBING

BANNER ELK, N.C.—Usually a person chooses between a college education or one at the school of hard knocks. However, in this small mountain town three adventurous youths have chosen to combine both curricula—they attend Lees-McRae College to gain a conventional education, and they scale vertical rock walls for experience and hard knocks.

Whenever the sun warms the air and the rocks are free of ice (and their classsroom duties fulfilled), Kevin Hollifield, Martin Richter and Sheldon Christy can be found spidering their way up the sheer cliffs that abound in the mountains surrounding their college.

On a recent sunny day, the trio visited one of their favorite spots—Ship Rock, located a short hike from the Blue Ridge Parkway. Carrying a rope and a backpack full of gear, Martin, Kevin and Sheldon climbed steadily among the tumbled boulders at the base of the huge escarpment as they chose from a selection of difficult vertical ascents.

Amputee, Special Forces, Hindu Kush, Harpoon, and The Anguish of Captain Bligh are names given to some of the routes up the ever varying vertical wall of Ship Rock. **The Climber's Guide to North Carolina** by Thomas Kelley lists and illlustrates fifty-eight routes for this one massive ledge.

"The climbers name a spot by what it reminds them of. Hindu Kush, with all those dihedrals sticking out, reminds you of the mountains in that range. That's why it's called Hindu Kush," said Martin, the most experienced of the climbers.

This day the students chose to climb Harpoon and The Anguish of Captain Bligh, two adjacent routes. On a scale of 5.0-5.3 Easy, 5.4-5.6 Moderate, 5.7-5.9 Difficult, and 5.10-5.13 Extremely Difficult, Harpoon is a 5.10 and Captain Bligh a 5.11.

"These climbs require everything you've got," said Martin.

"Yeah—balance, endurance, strength and flexibility," said Sheldon.

The equipment is not extensive, but it is important. Tough nylon webbing ("It'll support a car," said Sheldon), special climbing rope, carribiners (small metal loops to attach to the ropes and webbing), figure eights to run the rope through, chalk to keep fingers dry and climbing shoes.

"The shoes are made of rubber that sticks to the rock. We use Sportiva Megas; they're the best shoes for edging," said Sheldon.

One at a time the climbers ascend the cliff, fingers stretching for thin cracks, rubber-booted toes searching for bumps or crevices.

They are top rope climbing, the safest method. A rope is run through a carribiner attached to nylon webbing secured at the top of the cliff. One end of the rope is tied to a belt harness on the climber; the other is run through a figure eight attached to a tree while one of them (the belayer) keeps the rope tight as his friend climbs.

If the climber loses his battle with gravity, the rope prevents his falling to the rocks below, and the belayer lowers him gently down.

"Climbing is very life-threatening if a climber is careless or neglectful of safety. Even the best climbers may have a serious accident due to not double-checking their equipment," said Kevin.

"Solo climbing is the most dangerous type of climbing. Only professionals should attempt it. A climber uses no equipment such as a rope and harness. If he falls, he will fall to his death," said Sheldon.

The dangers are obvious. So why cimb rocks?

"For me climbing is a natural high, and there's no way to explain the feeling of accomplishing a tricky climb. Even with all the dangers, there's no way I'll give it up," said Kevin.

"It's personal achievement, too. You can always do better," said Martin.

Two friends arrived in the middle of the climbing. Heidi Parker and Kelly. Heidi, who had climbed before, gave it a try again, not to be outdone by the males, who encourage their friends to try their obsession.

When asked how the climbing affected their schoolwork, Sheldon immediately said, "I think it helps."

"You get a chance to get away from everything, and it's so peaceful. It's relaxing," said Kevin.

So the students/climbers will continue to spend part of their time inside the rock walls of Lees-McRae College improving their minds, and part of it clinging to the rock walls of nearby mountains, literally expanding their horizons.

OLD HAMPTON STORE AND GRIST MILL

LINVILLE, N.C.—In today's world of department stores stocked with market-researched merchandise and specialty stores devoted to a limited field, it is refreshing to find yourself in a store stocked as much by personal whim and nostalgia as by rational consideration.

Such a place is the Old Hampton Store and Grist Mill. Proprietor Jeffrey McManus and manager Cloudy Jackson have assembled a fascinating array of merchandise. A quick stop to pick up their stone-ground corn meal may turn into a lingering stay of exploration and memories.

For one thing there are the marbles. Even if you haven't wedged a shooter in front of your thumb's top joint for 30 years, reaching into a basket and pulling out a smooth, red cat's-eye will carry you back. You want to sink to your knees and send it flying. There are even marble bags to carry your spoils away in, for your children or grandchildren, of course.

And if you do give in and find that once on the floor you can't get up again too easily, within reach are some hand carved walking sticks to help you regain your feet with some grace.

For energy to help you in your efforts, there are lines of glass jars crammed full of candy—crystalline rock candy, licorice whips, and many others that you haven't seen in a decade or two.

Cast-iron pots, pans and muffin molds; blue, red and pastel enamelware; kerosene lamps and candle sticks; hiking, hunting and fishing supplies; boots, belt buckles, baskets and carriage bolts; even bag balm—the list goes on and on.

But the pride of the Old Hampton Store and Grist Mill is the grist products.

"Cast-iron, enamelware, even kerosene lamps you can find pretty easily anywhere, but our mill products are unique to this area. They are inspected by the North Carolina Department of Agriculture, and we guarantee them 100%," says Jeffrey McManus proudly.

"We grind cornmeal, both white and yellow; white and yellow grits, high protein whole wheat, pure buckwheat, and we also sell buckwheat pancake mix, pancake and waffle mix, and hush puppy mix," he says.

A grist mill was part of the Hampton Store when it first opened in 1921 to service the logging industry and local residents. The store was one of the original stops for the Tweetsie Railroad.

"The Tweetsie Railroad bed is my boundary line back here behind the grist mill," says McManus, pointing to a raised mound.

Old Hampton Store

In addition to the cornmeal, the store is famous for McManus' fresh breads.

"The original store closed down in 1965, and when I bought it in 1985 it was just a shell. I had the completely renovate it. I came across the mill parts and asked a local boy what they were. He explained how they made up the grist mill, and I decided to include that in my business," he says.

While the original mill was irreparable, McManus was able to buy a new Meadows Mill made in Wilkes County. It has 30-inch stones and is run by electricity.

"One thing I've found about milling is that you can grind on a 200-year-old water mill or a brand new electric mill; what makes the difference is the quality of the corn. If you grind good corn, you get good meal.

"W. C. Linneys from Alexander County taught me all I know about milling. He's 74 years old, and he's been in the milling business a long time. I rely on W.C. to gauge the quality of the corn. He buys it locally and he always gets superior corn. That's our edge in the milling business," says McManus.

He runs his mill when his stock gets low, not on a schedule. Because he uses no pesticides or insecticides on the product, he needs to keep it fresh; according to McManus, "When we're out of meal, we run it."

So while you might not get to see the mill in operation, you can be sure of getting a fresh bag.

"I sell between 40,000-50,000 pounds a year. It's a good product and something that we're proud of. We want our grist products to be the thing which our reputation is built on. I'm not looking for a $50 sale from each customer. If someone buys a bag of meal, I'm happy," he says.

The Old Hampton Store and Grist Mill is located about two miles from the intersection of highways 221 and 181 in Linville, North Carolina, less than five miles from Grandfather Mountain and the Blue Ridge Parkway. Store hours are 11-5 weekdays.

If you like a corn bread that tastes like fresh, sweet corn, stop in and buy a bag of the yellow cornmeal. But don't be surprised if you spend more time there than money.

Jeff McManus with cornmeal ground at the store's grist mill.

A flying squirrel peaks out of one of Weigl's boxes.

NORTHERN FLYING SQUIRRELS

ROAN MOUNTAIN—The Saturday morning on Roan Mountain was cold, temperatures in the single digits and snow knee-deep with drifts over the waist.

The only creatures stirring before the skiers arrived were the Northern Flying Squirrels and Pete Weigl and his team who are studying this rare denizen of the Roan.

Why study the Northern Flying Squirrel, especially under such conditions?

"It's an animal that's very rare and sporadic in distribution. There's a concern about losing this sub-species," said Weigl, a Wake Forest University biology professor.

The squirrels, nocturnal animals that live in the high elevation forests of the Southeast, are another piece in the puzzle of the forest death syndrome that is devastating these mountaintop forests.

"We are running out of time to study this squirrel. Before we can begin to understand it, its habitat may be gone," said Weigl.

While a number of projects are attempting to discover the causes of the disastrous forest decline throughout the Southern Appalachians, only Weigl's is looking at its effect on an animal.

"This is an indicator species; anything that affects the habitat will affect this species. By studying the Northern Flying Squirrels we will in effect be studying the health of other animals living in the same area," said Weigl.

In addition to its role as an indicator species, the Northern Flying Squirrel is interesting in itself.

"The animal has some intrinsically interesting characteristics, such as its diet and its survival in this extreme climate. Its distribution is sporadic over these islands of high elevation; therefore its evolutionary history is intriguing. There's the question of the genetics of these small, isolated groups," said Weigl.

Joining Weigl in his work are Alan Smith and Travis Knowles, who on this day were learning the locations of the squirrels and trying out the equipment to keep track of them.

"Their habitat is an ecotone, the blending zone of hardwoods and spruce-fir forests," said Smith, a consulting biologist from Mars Hill, North Carolina.

Deep in this ecotone, the squirrels are captured by trapping them in nesting boxes that are placed in trees to attract the squirrels. Not every box has a squirrel at home, so collecting them is not easy.

"Over the past two years we've caught close to 30 animals. They're an endangered sub-species, so they're difficult to gather," said Weigl.

Once caught, the squirrels are weighed and measured, then tags are inserted in their ears by the team members. Before release, the squirrels get electronic transmitters placed around their necks.

"All our squirrels have pierced ears and now they'll have collars. Keep in mind these are flying squirrels, they glide, so this gear doesn't weigh much," said Weigl.

The freed squirrels immediately dash up their home trees, some jumping in the nesting box, others soaring gracefully away from the intruders.

This was the first time the transmitters were tried. They are commercially designed, and a "real improvement" over the past, more limited transmitters, according to Weigl.

"It's called radio telemetry. The transmitter responds to heat by increasing the pulse rate, which the receiver picks up; this tells whether the squirrels are warm in their nesting box or out in the cold," said Travis Knowles, a former graduate student of Weigl, who is getting his feet wet, literally, on this project.

As he stood in the snow, pointing the antenna toward the tree where two squirrels had just been released, he explained, "That'll give us information about what they're doing—huddling in the nest or out and about; also we'll know where they are."

The transmitters provide data about the squirrels' movements and the amount of territory they cover. By recording this information, the researchers will create a database about the behavior and biological and territorial needs of this endangered sub-species.

"We'll generate a lot of work for graduate students and biologists for years to come. Also, the Forest Service will be able to more rationally manage the species," said Weigl.

The project is sponsored by the North Carolina Wildlife Commission and utilizes the resources of several groups.

"I work with the Southern Appalachian Highlands Conservancy, the North Carolina Nature Conservancy, the North Carolina Wildlife Resources Commission, and the local people," said Weigl.

"It's critical to know the people that live on the mountain. They tell you things about the place, and they're the ones to help protect the mountain. Getting to know them has been a worthwhile experience over the years. I'd rather work on Roan Mountain than elsewhere," he said.

For 24 years Weigl has been coming to this mountain and to mountains throughout the Southern Appalachians to study the flying squirrels.

Dr. Peter Weigl (right) and his assistant with an antenna.

Today his research carries with it the growing recognition that slow death is death nonetheless.

"This species may be the first affected by the die-off of the forests. When something kills the forest, this animal will show the signs early, and certainly we'll lose it," he says.

While some researchers look for easy answers to the forest death, Weigl recognizes that the problem is far reaching.

"Acid rain is only part of the problem; heavy metal deposition is equally bad, and there are other kinds of pollutants that settle on the mountains. To halt the problem we need a major change in our thinking that will affect our use of energy for development and for lifestyle. The leadership has been lacking in environmental thought," Weigl says.

Despite his worries, or perhaps because of them, the biologist carries on his work to contribute his bits of knowledge to complete the confounding puzzle.

Neither rain, nor snow . . . .

BALD MOUNTAINS

Set among the majestic mountains of the Southern Appalachians are a number of special jewels, the emerald balds.

Mystery shrouds the origin of these treeless, grassy meadows in the sky, just as the clouds and mist often obscure them from eyes below. Written records of this area extend only to the 18th century, except for accounts from the travels of DeSoto in the 16th century, beyond which time conjecture replaces fact.

Who or what created them? When? Why? And why have they remained bald?

Many different theories have been advanced to explain the origin of the balds.

The highest peaks in the area are forested. Mount Mitchell, the highest mountain east of the Mississippi, has its spruce-fir forest. So the balds are obviously not above the timberline. Reasons other than mere height alone must be sought to explain the lack of trees.

Some explanations credit nature with the clearing of the balds. Natural fires caused by lightning, which often strikes high elevation trees, is one proposed explanation.

Another is that extensive ice and frost damage to the exposed heights could have created clearings. Also the destructive action of high winds, or infestations by oak gall wasps could be responsible. In addition, soil characteristics have been cited as contributing to the lack of woody vegetation.

Climatic changes could have created the balds. Spruce-fir forests couldn't grow on the lower peaks following the glacial period, because the climate became too warm; and only the highest, coldest peaks could sustain such growth. Centuries later when the climate cooled again, there was no seed source to create a forest on the lower, warmer mountain tops; therefore these peaks remained open and grassy.

Of course, man may have created the balds. One theory maintains that the Cherokees cleared the trees from the peaks to form hunting areas and lookout posts.

Some balds are known to have been created by white settlers as grazing ranges for their livestock during the mid-19th century. Interviews with longtime residents of the Great Smoky Mountains have verified that certain landowners cleared ridgetops for this purpose.

"It seems impossible in most cases to determine exactly what caused the trees to be removed from balds, and it seems fairly reasonable to suppose that different factors could be important in different places," writes Mary Lindsay in her study, **The Vegetation of the Grassy Balds and Other High Elevation Disturbed Areas in Great Smoky Mountains National Park**.

Each bald has its own history, and the different soil characteristics of each site obviously affect the vegetation growth.

Bob Carey, district ranger for the Toecane District, believes the balds predated the appearance of the white man.

"Balds were here when settlers first arrived," he says. "My own conjecture from studying information written by early explorers such as Lawson and Bartram is that many of the balds may have been the result of Indian burning.

"Also, the changes in climate may have cleared some before the Indians," he says, "but the balds were here before the whites."

Cherokee legends refer to the balds, saying that they were cleared by lightning and fire sent by the Great Spirit to destroy immense, evil birds who carried off the children of the Indians.

While some discount the importance of such legends, claiming Indian traditions were short-lived and adapted to fit the local landscape, others argue that the tradition suggests an ancient history for the balds.

After the question of their origin comes that of why the balds have remained clear of woody vegetation.

Most experts agree grazing kept the trees from returning to the balds. Before the white settlers arrived, large herds of elk, deer, and buffalo roamed the mountains.

"Elk, buffalo, and deer would naturally have grazed the high meadows," explains Carey. "Their activity would have maintained the balds until the settlers arrived."

"Then the settlers grazed their herds on them," he says. "Up until the government purchased Round Bald up from Carver's Gap, it was regularly grazed."

Research conducted by Ms. Lindsay in the Great Smoky Mountains National Park documents the extensive use of balds by farmers for grazing their livestock from the late 18th century until the establishment of the park in 1936.

Each year between April and May, cows, sheep, mules, and horses would be driven from as far away as 60 miles to the balds where a herder received about a dollar a head to look after them, to provide salt, to round up any strays, and to kill any bears that might endanger the animals.

In addition, some individual families maintained their own small herds on ridges near their land.

During September when the herds were rounded up and sorted out, a general festival would be held on the balds. Then the owners would drive the herds to market in Knoxville, Tennessee, or back to their farms.

With the creation of the park, grazing has ended for domestic animals; no large herds of elk, buffalo, or deer remain, and park rangers prevent fires—so the park balds have begun to change.

Today the fear is that without management the balds will revert to forest in less than a hundred years.

"The balds are a really important resource," Carey points out. "If they grow up, some rare and endangered species could disappear from this area.

"Already we are losing some of the important mountain oat grass to blackberries that have emerged since grazing stopped, and Gray's Lily, which is extremely rare and grows on the Roan Massif, would be lost.

"The wildlife of the balds would suffer too, if they were allowed to grow up," he says. "The golden eagles and peregrine falcons which are being reintroduced in this area need the open areas provided by the grassy balds to hunt. Roan ravens would suffer too."

Another important consideration is the value of the balds to hikers, campers, skiers, and other outdoor enthusiasts. The open views attract many to the balds at all seasons of the year, for they present a visual experience very different from that of forested mountains. The eye can roam for miles and miles, unobstructed by the vegetation.

To preserve the balds, several techniques are being considered and used by government agencies. Their options include mowing, grazing, hand cutting, and using fire. There is some disagreement about the use of herbicides, for poisoning the balds to preserve them is a shortsighted approach.

"We've been working on burning to keep Round Bald open for about four years," says Carey.

On Beauty Spot in Unicoi County, Tennessee, mowing has proven effective. The easy access and gentle slopes of this well-known bald make machine mowing practical.

Grazing is being used by the Southern Appalachian Highlands Conservancy on Yellow Mountain, a part of the Roan Massif. Also, a large area of the Jefferson National Forest in Virginia is being grazed by ponies.

According to Ms. Lindsay, "No public complaints about grazing stock or fences have been noted, except that a few hikers have complained about being intimidated by pony stallions."

Finally, hand cutting is the method used to preserve the Roan Gardens.

"Volunteers are a big help in the cutting program," says Carey. "One local nursery owner has helped to keep the gardens in good shape. Volunteers are important to us.''

The balds, special gems in the mountains of the Southeast, provide a glimpse into the past, as well as incomparable views of our world today. Careful study and care will ensure that they will be open for years to come to provide such sights for future generations.

Full moon rises over balds of Roan Massif.

BURNSVILLE

BURNSVILLE, N.C.—Once called "The Gem City of the Mountains," Burnsville still presents a jewel-like appearance. Centered on a well-kept acre of green, the town is set in the ring of high mountains which surround the county.

Even before the land west of the Blue Ridge was officially opened to white settlers in 1778, a few hardy families had established themselves in the Toe River Valley. By 1833 when Yancey was formed from parts of Buncombe and Burke counties, a thriving mountain culture existed in the valley.

One of the area's leading citizens, the hot-tempered "Yellow Jacket" John Bailey, offered a 100-acre tract of land on a plateau near the center of the county to become its seat. By March 1834, the land was secured by the commissioners.

The name "Burnsville" was chosen not because Capt. Otway Burns was an important local figure, but because this naval hero of the War of 1812 persistently supported the movement in the North Carolina General Assembly to create the new county.

In 1909 a statue of Burns was erected on a 40-ton granite pedestal in the center of the town square. On the pedestal is a plaque which states in part, "He Guarded Well Our Seas, Let Our Mountains Honor Him."

While his sword and bugle have been removed several times and he stands without them today, his copper form has dominated the square throughout this century.

After the naming of the town, creating public buildings became a prime concern. Some of the acreage secured from Bailey was sold to finance the brick courthouse which was in operation by the fall of 1836. In 1908 a new courthouse was erected on the corner of the square and continues to house city offices.

Throughout the 19th century, Burnsville served as the center of the county's business, which was largely agricultural, as well as its political, educational, and legal systems. Later, the timber harvests and the growing mineral industry also contributed to the town's prosperity.

Men and women looked to a visit to the county seat as a chance to forget the day-to-day struggle for life on the farms.

With the difficulties in transporting goods to market, often the corn and apples would be turned into liquor and brandy, a gallon jug being easier to carry than a couple of bushels.

"Fighting and drinking seem to have been among the most common sports, and the two usually went together," wrote Jason Deyton in **The Toe River Valley to 1865**.

According to Deyton, in the spring term of Superior Court in 1837, 10 of the 14 cases tried were for assault and battery or for affray. In the fall term of 1840, 31 of 55 cases were for the same.

The meeting of the court was always an excuse for carousing.

In 1854 Judge Merrimon, who traveled from Asheville to preside, expressed his anger and indignation at the conditions:

"Little of importance has occurred today. There has been a goodeal of noise kept up round a liquor wagon. . . . I feel confident in saying that I have never seen a court behave so badly and keep such confusion. . . . At different times I noticed groups about over the Court Yard and in the center stood a large gauky looking fellow with a fiddle and he would saw off some silly ditty two or three drunken fools would dance to the same."

Despite the Judge's rancor, Burnsville represented more than simply commerce and carousing; education has always been a primary concern for the county's citizens.

In the 1840s the first public schools were established, and Burnsville Academy was founded. The academy was the educational center of the county for 50 years and operated on tuition.

"Teachers accepted as pay anything of value that they needed—grain, flour, meal, bacon, poultry, honey, beeswax, deer hams, garments, homespun cloth, and a great many other articles," wrote James Hutchins, former superintendent of Yancey County schools.

As were many counties of Western North Carolina, Yancey was bitterly divided by the Civil War, and Burnsville was the scene of armed conflict.

In 1864, 75 men attacked the Confederate Home Guard in Burnsville, breaking into the magazine and taking all the arms and ammunition, then appropriating 500 pounds of bacon from the commissary.

"In the same locality, fifty women assembled and carried off an estimated sixty bushels of wheat," writes Wilma Dykeman in **The French Broad**.

Even after the war, ill feelings persisted, with a former Union private being indicted at Burnsville in 1867 for actions committed while he was acting under orders. The Ku Klux Klan also operated in the area for several years.

When novelist Charles Dudley Warner visited the city in 1885, life had resumed its normal course of agricultural and business pursuits augmented by an embryonic tourist trade.

"The country around Burnsville is not only mildly picturesque, but very pleasing. Burnsville at an elevation of 2,840 feet is more like a New England village than any hitherto seen. Most of the houses stand about a square, which contains the shabby courthouse; around it are two small churches, a jail, an inviting tavern, with a long veranda, and a couple of stores," writes Warner.

The "inviting tavern" still operates today as the Nu-Wray Inn. It was originally established in the early 1800s, and despite changing hands a couple times, continues to house and feed visitors to the city while holding a national reputation for the excellence of its mountain-style cuisine.

Warner found, "The elevation of Burnsville gives it a delightful summer climate, the gentle undulations of the country are agreeable, the views noble, the air is good, and it is altogether a 'liveable' and attractive place. With facilities of communication, it would be a favorite summer resort."

His description of a sleepy Sunday captures the typical calm of the city. "Sunday was a hot and quiet day. The stores were closed and the two churches also, this not being the Sunday for the itinerant preacher. The jail also showed no sign of life, and when we asked about it, we learned that it was empty and had been for some time."

During the week, county residents could find much commercial activity in Burnsville. There were six dry goods stores, several boots and harness shops, four blacksmith stands, three tanyards, a drugstore, dressmakers, lawyers, and doctors.

In 1896 Burnsville's first newspaper was established. *The Black Mountain Eagle* was published and edited by brothers-in-law J. M. Lyon and O. R. Lewis, whose partnership lasted for 40 years until the two men retired. Since then the weekly paper, *The Yancey Record*, and later *The Yancey Journal*, has been published by various owners.

As the schools, papers, and churches filed the rough edges off the citizenry, alcohol became less popular, at least during election time.

"In 1908, when the state voted on the prohibition question, there were only eleven votes cast in Yancey County against prohibition, and it now has the banner hanging in the court house given by the Temperance Women of North Carolina to the county casting the smallest vote in favor of whiskey," according to a pamphlet issued by the teacher training class of Burnsville in 1930.

Prohibition continues in Yancey County to this day, with attempts to repeal it always being stopped short of the ballot.

With the coming of the Black Mountain Railroad in 1912 and the construction of good roads in the last 30 years, Burnsville has become more accessible and enjoys a tourist industry such as that envisioned by Warner a century ago; however, many of the townspeople hope to preserve the natural beauty and easy pace that are their county's main attractions.

The past continues to linger about the Burnsville town square, and visitors are welcome to sample a taste of well-preserved mountain life.

HUGH MORTON—
GRANDFATHER'S GRANDFATHER

GRANDFATHER MOUNTAIN, N.C.—In Hugh Morton's office on Grandfather Mountain is a sign. It says, "Everything cometh to he who waiteth so long as he who waiteth worketh like hell while he waiteth."

The message is one that Morton has taken to heart throughout his life, and one that bodes well for the success of a project he has recently undertaken.

As the guardian of one of the most spectacular mountains in the Eastern United States, Morton has become aware of the gradually accelerating decline of mountaintop forests in the Southeast in particular, but all over the world in general.

And he is going to do something about it. With the help of writer Tom Sieg and independent television producer David Solomon, both of Winston-Salem, North Carolina, Morton is working on an hour-long Public Broadcasting Service special about the problem.

"We're rosy-cheeked do-gooders who have decided that, by gosh, we're going to do something about this. I may not be able to save the top of Grandfather Mountain, but I hope to preserve the lake in front of my house," says Morton.

That lake is what triggered the crusade. A visitor to Morton's mountaintop had gone to his lakefront house lower on Grandfather to be floated to an island in the lake where injured eagles were attempting to reproduce.

"As we crossed the lake with its trout—we have all three varieties— and other wildlife, she admired the beauty, saying it was like a lake she loved in the Adirondacks that is now dead, killed by acid rain. No fish, not even a crawfish. That started me thinking," says Morton.

With many people today, thinking is all that gets done when they are faced with a seemingly insurmountable problem; however, with Morton, the thinking led directly to action. He has been gathering authoritative information about the pollution problems, particularly that of acid rain.

"We are going to see, by God, that people are aware of the problem and that something can be done about it," he says.

First Morton looked into the local situation.

"I found that the tremendous deterioration on Mount Mitchell's spruce-fir forests has happened largely in the past five years. That really shook me up. The most acidic reading that Robert Bruck, who is heading up research in the Black Mountains, has obtained happened during rime ice. It was 2.1 on the ph scale; not far from 1.9 which is the reading on battery acid.

"The tender young growth is burned back by the acid. If that happens one or two years, you've got a dead tree. This is what is affecting our balsam and red spruce on our higher elevations," he says.

Bruck further said that there is 200 pounds per acre per year of sulfuric acid deposition on Mount Mitchell. Nature can accommodate at best 18 pounds per acre per year.

"That's more than 10 times the amount. It's that sort of thing that makes you wonder about people who refuse to see the problem," he says.

Morton also discovered that Charlotte Speedway spends $250,000 a year to correct problems caused by acid rain, that the coastal marshes with their shrimp, fish and birds are being affected by acid rain, that the outdoor sculptures at Biltmore House are deteriorating rapidly because of acid rain, and that new car dealers in Asheville have to buff out pits caused by acid rain in the finish of their new cars.

"I've had people say that they're sorry for me on the ridgetop. That acid rain's my problem. They don't realize that it's everybody's problem," he says.

Morton and his associates have already traveled to Canada to obtain firsthand information about the problems with acid rain that that country has experienced and to learn how the Canadians have started to reverse the damage to their lakes and forests.

"We met with their forestry people, medical experts, and some from their state department. They gave us a thorough briefing and took us on a guided tour. In the Province of Quebec there are 30,000 dead lakes. In the province of Ontario, 12,000 more dead lakes."

"If we had been at war we couldn't have done more damage and devastation to their environment," he says.

However, not all the news was bad. Morton discovered that the Canadians themselves have made substantial progress in reducing sulfuric acid emissions from their industries, cutting by 85% the pollution from the Sudbury area which had the worst problem in the country.

"If it wasn't something I thought we could do something about, I'd leave it alone. If the plants in Canada can do it, there are a whole lot of others that can," says Morton.

Already he has gotten a good response from those who have seen the slide show he has put together to present the problem to the public. Both individual citizens and public officials, such as Governor Martin of North Carolina, have been strongly moved by his graphic presentation. But Morton wants more.

"I want the average man on the street to recognize the problem. Congress doesn't lead; it follows. We want to make everyone aware of the dangers so that the pressure is there to do something."

"When the ordinary bass fisherman realizes that the pleasures of his life will be denied his son and grandson, he'll demand something be done," says Morton.

The production that he is working on for PBS will be authoritative and factual, based on irrefutable scientific evidence. Morton and his associates are hard at work gathering the data which will form the framework for the show.

While many environmentalists wring their hands in despair, Morton has rolled up his sleeves and gone to work.

"We need to do something, NOW," he says.

Hugh Morton beside the statue of Mildred the bear and her cubs.

LOGGING WITH HORSES

BULADEAN, N.C.—Dragging logs from the steep slopes of the high mountains is not an easy task, especially when done by real horse power, but for the traditionally independent mountaineer it offers an alternative to the mill work that pales the skin and deadens the soul.

As soon as the snow melted and the ground thawed, Grady Thomas and Jerry Putman, native sons of this rural community on the border of Tennessee, hitched up Pearl and headed into the woods near Hughes Gap to get out the locust trees to split for posts.

"Usually people don't want locust stakes after the sap gets up. Way up here it don't come up till April," said Grady, Pearl's master.

Among those who know, there is nothing that adequately replaces the locust post. It has the beauty of a natural wood and a legendary durability.

"A locust post will last you a lifetime, and that's about all you can ask," said Grady as he turned Pearl for another climb up the steep trail into the woods.

"There's nobody much into it anymore. You can start cutting them, and they will find you out. The man who buys ours comes from way above Abingdon, Virginia. He comes down here to pick them up," he said.

The work is not easy for man or horse. Just the climb up the slope raises the pulse and pops the perspiration.

"Folks have got too lazy. That's why they're dropping like flies with heart attacks and strokes. This work will fix that— blowing out the pipes is what I call it. You make a couple of trips up here and you'll know what I mean," said Grady, resting his mare halfway up the steepest part of the trail.

In addition to the benefits of an outdoor job and the physical exercise, independence is an important part of the work.

"What I like about it is working for yourself. You're your own boss," said Jerry Putman, a lifelong horseman whose earliest memories are about horses and hard work.

"Ever since I been able, I'd follow my father to everywhere he had to work. I'd ride in on the horse to work, and in the evening I'd get to ride him back," he said.

Nostalgia and an anachronistic love of beasts aside, logging with horses has its benefits for the land.

"When you take a horse in the woods on steep mountains, it don't tear up the woods like machines do," said Grady.

Grady Thomas and Jerry Putman logging with Pearl.

"Yeah, we're just getting into it. People who have some timber but don't want to tear it all up by bulldozers or skidders will let a horse in," said Jerry.

Although it is a soft technology, knowledge of the horse and the wood is necessary for the welfare of both man and beast. A 1600-1700 pound mare dragging a ton or two of long logs on steep land presents many problems for the horse master.

"They don't roll too bad going straight down the hill like this, but they do slide on you. If you try to go around the hill, then you've got to watch it.

"Also you got to be careful not to get caught between the logs or against a tree," said Grady.

Balance, flexibility, and agility are necessary for the man holding the driving lines. The mare gathers speed, the logs shift and swing, and trees beside the trail crowd in.

Quick reflexes are the difference between a good run down the hill and a trip to the hospital.

In addition there is the care and guidance of the horse. Special shoes must be made by welding on extra metal to serve as cleats to give the horse traction, but more importantly, special knowledge of the beast and its needs and temperament allows the master and his mare to work as one.

"I just treat her like I'd want to be treated myself if I was hooked up," said Grady. "I feed her good, and watch to not overwork her."

No one gets rich logging with horses, but the work is its own reward, as well as providing the basic necessities for the workers.

"As long as you've got food, clean water, clean air, and a place to live, money don't mean nothing. Peace of mind, that's what's important," said Grady, taking off Pearl's harness after the day's work.

A hundred years ago his great grandfather may well have said the same words while performing the same actions.

Pearl with two stout locust logs.